Haunted
Hudson Valley

Ghosts and Strange Phenomena of New York's Sleepy Hollow Country

Cheri Farnsworth

Illustrations by Marc Radle

STACKPOLE BOOKS

0 11557 03621 3

Published by
STACKPOLE BOOKS
5067 Ritter Road
Mechanicsburg, PA 17055
www.stackpolebooks.com

Printed the United States

10 9 8 7 6 5 4 3 2 1

FIRST EDITION

Cover design by Tessa Sweigert
Author photo on page 121 by Jamie Revai

Library of Congress Cataloging-in-Publication Data

Farnsworth, Cheri, 1963–
      Haunted Hudson Valley : ghosts and strange phenomena of New York's Sleepy Hollow country / Cheri Farnsworth ; illustrations by Marc Radle. — 1st ed.
          p.   cm.
      Includes bibliographical references (p.   ).
      ISBN-13: 978-0-8117-3621-3 (pbk.)
      ISBN-10: 0-8117-3621-0 (pbk.)
      1. Ghosts—Hudson River Valley (N.Y. and N.J.) 2. Haunted places—Hudson River Valley (N.Y. and N.J.) 3. Curiosities and wonders—Hudson River Valley (N.Y. and N.J.) I. Title.
  BF1472.U6F34 2010
  133.109747'3—dc22

2009040866

To my dear grandparents
Germaine and the late Elwood Dishaw
Je t'aime.

Contents

Introduction

A drowsy, dreamy influence seems to hang over the land, and to pervade the very atmosphere . . . the place still continues under the sway of some witching power, that holds a spell over the minds of the good people, causing them to walk in a continual reverie. They are given to all kinds of marvelous beliefs, are subject to trances and visions, and frequently see strange sights, and hear music and voices in the air.

Washington Irving
"The Legend of Sleepy Hollow" (1820)

WHATEVER YOU DO, DON'T DRIVE THROUGH THE HUDSON VALLEY! LET someone else do the driving so you can watch the roadside and the sky and the distant tree line. The area is a popular hotspot for supernatural sightings; Bigfoot has been seen and videotaped near a campsite and a pair of large, black phantom cats has been encountered in the woods along the Palisades Parkway and in Tallman Mountain State Park. Whatever your destination, your itinerary should include stops at some of our nation's most haunted places. After all, this is Sleepy Hollow Country, a region synonymous with the supernatural.

The Hudson Valley contains the towns and cities on either side of New York's Hudson River, from northern Westchester County and the suburbs of New York City all the way up to Albany. The river Indians, Mahican and Munsee tribes, were the first people believed to occupy the valley; but studies of the mysterious stone chambers throughout Putnam County beg for reconsideration of that long-held hypothesis, as you'll see later. We do know with certainty, however, when the first Europeans arrived, thanks to ancient records and accounts that have somehow survived various disasters, such as the great fire in the state's capitol that left countless other original documents in ashes and a night watchman dead (but he's still around). In the 1610s, Dutch settlers established a trading post on the Hudson River, just south of Albany; from that point on, the population increased steadily along the Hudson Valley corridor. Although the Hudson Valley figured prominently in the American Revolution, during which it was one of the major areas of conflict, it wasn't truly put on the map and given supernatural status worldwide until Washington Irving released the most popular ghost story ever told, "The Legend of Sleepy Hollow." His famous tale, along with "Rip Van Winkle," was based on the Hudson Valley people and landmarks familiar to him. It was Irving's memorable words that immortalized the region's reputation of inherent spookiness.

The area enjoyed a period of industrialization in the 1800s, thanks to the construction of the Erie Canal. The city of Troy, in fact, has been dubbed "the birthplace of the Industrial Revolution." Many of its old factories have been transformed into lucrative new businesses, like the former Empire Stove Works factory, which now houses the haunted Irish Mist Restaurant. During that same period, wealthy industrialists and famous individuals chose to relocate to the Hudson Valley, building their mansions and sprawling estates on or near the famed river. Many of those estates have been meticulously maintained and carefully restored to the splendor of their heyday for the general public to enjoy.

The Hudson Valley is generally divided into three regions, but for the purposes of this book, I've given West Point its own section, although it technically resides in one of the Mid-Hudson counties. After all, wouldn't you expect the oldest of the five national service academies to be haunted, especially when its military garrison played such a key role in the Revolutionary War? The stories in this book are arranged from north to south: Upper Hudson, Mid-Hudson, West Point, and Lower Hudson.

I've written several books about ghosts of the Empire State— *The Big Book of New York Ghost Stories*, *Haunted New York*, *Haunted New York City*, and four volumes of *Haunted Northern*

Introduction

New York. Although the latter has consistently been worthy of multiple tomes (primarily because it's in my own backyard, so the stories seem to just appear on my doorstep), after writing this book, I've conceded that the Hudson Valley may be the single most haunted region in my home state. In terms of all things paranormal—UFOs, Bigfoot and other cryptid creatures, extraterrestrials, alien abductions, geological enigmas, and so on—the Hudson Valley is hands-down the most active area of the state. Irving was on the mark when he said, "The whole neighborhood abounds with local tales, haunted spots, and twilight superstitions; stars shoot and meteors glare oftener across the valley than in any other part of the country." Those words are as true today as they were nearly two hundred years ago when he wrote them. But were the celestial lights he spoke of really shooting stars and meteors, or has the Hudson Valley been visited by UFOs and subjected to extraterrestrial-related phenomena for far longer than we even imagined?

In a region where time seems to have stood still for millennia, where even the trees appear sleepy, and where a character named Rip Van Winkle could doze for twenty years, it's not surprising that Irving's legendary tales have endured. In a sense, not much has changed. The little towns still have an enchanted feel about them that is reminiscent of a setting from a Grimm's fairy tale. The Hudson Valley still has its tales, still has its haunted spots and superstitions, and still has lights that streak across the sky more often than in any other part of the country. Here you will read the best of the unusual, supernatural things so often experienced in this single 184-mile corridor of New York State.

Upper Hudson Valley

THE UPPER HUDSON VALLEY INCLUDES ALBANY AND RENSSELAER counties, with the cities of Albany and Troy. Besides the haunted New York State Capitol, this region's list of most haunted sites includes several colleges, a music hall, a restaurant, a coffeehouse, a cemetery, and three famous mansions. Although it may lack the UFO traffic enjoyed by its southern neighbors on either side of the Hudson in the villages of Pine Bush and Brewster, it has had at least one notable incident at the Albany International Airport, which yielded some pretty convincing UFO video footage.

Bull's Head Inn

While not technically within the Hudson Valley region, the town and village of Cobleskill are pretty darn close—only thirty-five minutes west of Albany. This story is included here because it's too good to pass up. Anyone roaming the countryside looking for Hudson Valley haunts could easily include the Bull's Head Inn as a stop on their itinerary.

In 1752, the year the village of Cobleskill was first settled, George Ferster built a log cabin at 2 Park Place in the district near Main Street. During the French and Indian War, the property sat amid murder and mayhem. One Indian took another's life inside

Ferster's log cabin. Then, when the village was invaded in 1778 by the Tories and Indians under Joseph Brant, the cabin was burned to the ground. William E. Roscoe wrote in his 1882 *History of Schoharie County*, "A messenger was dispatched on horseback down the valley to apprise the inhabitants of their danger of being slain or captured. . . . The dwelling of George Ferster, which stood where the Courter house now stands . . . [and] all within the immediate neighborhood, were but smoking ruins, and their occupants refugees in the cheerless forest." Imagine the horror and chaos, as women fled to the forest where they hid for days with their children, uncertain of when it would be safe to return home. Three years later, after a new log cabin had been built to replace the first, the Tories returned to the valley:

> In the latter part of September 1781, a party of Indians from the Mohawk appeared in the [same] neighborhood and were joined by a number of the Tories to carry out their designs. . . . They crept slyly to the valley unperceived and began the work of devastation in burning Lawrence Lawyer's, John Bouck's, George Ferster's, and John King's house, that had been rudely rebuilt after the invasion of 1778.

After his second log cabin was destroyed, Ferster built a tavern there, which he sold to Lambert Lawyer. When Lawyer's tavern burned to the ground in 1802, the Federal-Georgian structure that still stands today was built by a well-respected carpenter named Seth Wakeman. It was then that the tavern became the Bull's Head Inn and simultaneously served as village courthouse and town hall.

When prosperous businessman Charles Courter strode into town in 1837, he married into another prominent family, the Lawyers, and purchased the Bull's Head Inn to convert back into a private residence. Who was going to argue with the man who was quickly elected to the county's Board of Supervisors, became president of the First National Bank of Cobleskill, and founded the village's Lutheran church? Courter lived at the Bull's Head Inn for just over four decades, until he became ill during a business trip, returned home, and died of pneumonia on New Year's Day in 1879.

The next notable occupants were John Stacy and his wife, who was his polar opposite. The Stacys arrived at the house in 1920. Mr. Stacy loved his booze as much as his wife abhorred it; the first irony of their story is that John Stacy became known as a village lush, while Mrs. Stacy was so opposed to alcohol that she became a staunch member of the Women's Christian Temperance Union (WCTU). This was at a time when "normally quiet housewives dropped to their knees in pray-ins in local saloons and demanded that the sale of liquor be stopped," according to the WCTU website. Such an irreconcilable difference of opinion between the husband and wife may explain why Mrs. Stacy slept in her own room. This leads us to the second irony of the Stacys' story.

Monty Allen purchased the property in 1966 and reopened it as a tavern, once again calling it the Bull's Head Inn. And guess where the bar was set up? In Mrs. Stacy's old bedroom! Certainly, she began stirring in her grave. Subsequent owner Bob Youngs kicked it up a notch, establishing a microbrewery on the premises before selling the place to the next owners, who continued operating it as a pub and eatery.

The majority of reported paranormal activity began when the house was converted back into an inn. Since then, owners, customers, managers, and bartenders have all experienced the wrath of a presence that is presumably Mrs. Stacy. Objects like ashtrays and wineglasses fly off tables, doors slam shut, dishes and silverware levitate, and napkins get moved around. Lights turn on and off inexplicably, as do water faucets and, once, even an unplugged cappuccino machine. Similarly, disconnected old-style telephones have reportedly been heard ringing. Though everything is tidied up before the last person leaves for the night, chairs have been found out of place the next morning.

It is assumed that the culprit is Mrs. Stacy. Why? For one thing, a former manager reported seeing an apparition of a woman in the mirrors. Also, customers and employees have seen a woman wearing a long, white old-fashioned gown gliding through the dining room and sitting in a rocking chair in the ladies' room, appearing as authentic as a restroom attendant. Mostly, the apparition is white, misty, and transparent, taking a decidedly feminine form as it disappears effortlessly through solid walls and tables or hovers near the bar in the basement.

Today, the Bull's Head Inn is owned by Tony Giammattei, who told Capital News 9 that he found the landmark restaurant abandoned by its previous owners and the "tables overturned." Who

turned the tables upside down? Did the former owners walk in one morning to find them that way—like the chairs they always found moved—prompting them to make a hasty departure? Or did the resident ghosts turn them over between owners out of sheer boredom? At any rate, Mr. Giammattei is fine with the restaurant's spooky reputation and, according to head chef Bill Thetford, plans to turn the Bull's Head Inn into an upscale steak house that the community can be proud of.

The Whining in West Hall

On July 10, 1897, a *New York Times* correspondent from Troy reported that a day earlier, an ill-fated peddler named George Horan died at the Troy Hospital, and a witness, Charles A. Pixley, said that Horan had been murdered by the night watchman at the institution, Philip Crossen. "At the Coroner's inquest, several witnesses testified that Crossen, the keeper, had strapped Horan to a cot and beaten him in the face with a strap, after which he left him uncared for until he died Tuesday night."

The former hospital is now West Hall, which today houses Rensselaer Polytechnic Institute's (RPI) arts department, several offices, and the Rensselaer Music Association—and is the campus's most haunted building. Located on Eighth Street in Troy, West Hall served as the Troy Hospital from about 1869 to 1914. Construction of the stately Second Empire building began in 1868 at the behest of the Sisters of Charity of Saint Vincent de Paul, who operated the facility with an unusual stance of taking in anyone in need, regardless of economic class, ethnic background, or religious affiliation. In that forty-five-year stint as a hospital, the building's walls absorbed the energy of untold human suffering on a daily basis, with people being brought in dying of incurable illnesses, tragic accidents, cold-blooded assaults, and old age. As a hospital, it was a place to go to be healed or die; a repository for drunks, bums, and other social misfits; and an alternative facility for the insane. As compassionate as the Sisters were in this magnificent building, the Troy Hospital was not a happy place. The inmates, as the patients were called, faced their greatest fears of death, disability, dementia, destitution, or abandonment.

Since at least 1985, the West Hall ghost has been highly publicized, beginning in RPI's own newspaper with the article "Is Betsy Roaming West Hall?" Eric Lambiaso told of a nurse believed to be from the Civil War era named Betsy, who allegedly went on a maniacal murdering spree while tending to the insane patients in the basement. The widespread legend had her "doing away with" the more troublesome patients on the midnight shift, and it's said she continues to scare people to this day, haunting West Hall by flushing its toilets, slamming its doors, and wailing or whining. There's no documentation that patients were murdered on Nurse Betsy's watch, although at least one patient, George Horan, was beaten to death by a night watchman, as described above. Furthermore, the 1880 census for the institute revealed no one by the name of Betsy or Betty or anything of that nature living or working there; but, the 1900 census lists a twenty-four-year-old Bessie McMahon living at the hospital as a housekeeper. Of all the female names listed, that was the only name remotely similar to Betsy. Perhaps our Betsy is really a Bessie—or even a Bertha. In 1899, a young woman named Bertha Hughes was found at four o'clock in the morning, lying on nearby railroad tracks with a severed leg and arm after being struck by the Montreal Express. She was taken to the Troy Hospital and died five hours later. Could she be the spirit heard moaning over the years? Then again, when you think about it, nearly everyone who ever entered the facility's doors probably had a pretty good reason to moan and complain.

Following its use as a hospital, the building sat vacant for several years, during which vandals and thieves left their marks, as did Mother Nature. During World War I, the U.S. War Office restored the structure sufficiently to use as a training facility and barracks, but they had been in it for only a short time before the armistice ending the war in 1918 was signed and the building was deserted once again. In 1923, the Albany Roman Catholic Diocese purchased it, renovated it to accommodate school rooms like a gymnasium and cafeteria, and opened it in 1925 to serve five hundred Catholic students. In twenty-five years, the student population had tripled, and the diocese was forced to find a larger school for their needs. In 1952, RPI purchased the fortress to house offices, classrooms, and laboratories, and it was officially named West Hall, for its location on the campus's west side, a year later. In 1991, a massive multimillion dollar restoration project was approved, but work had barely gotten under way when the project was canceled (to be resurrected in 2004). It had apparently been enough to awaken the dead, for that's when West Hall's ghost stories began in earnest.

The night custodians complained of hearing doors closing and opening in empty hallways, glass breaking for which no sources could be found, and eerie, far-off screams. Printers and other office machines have been known to come on by themselves. The custodians have even complained of smelling fresh-baked cookies, but never being able to find them. (Now that's a valid complaint!) Such reports were corroborated by a couple of students who volunteered to spend the night in the basement, where the hospital's insane patients were purportedly housed, to see if they heard anything unusual. Imagine the excitement generated when they captured a "three-second whine" on tape that they hadn't heard with their own ears. Once, as two individuals tried to open a door, they actually heard someone moaning on the other side. Rather than check to see that no one was hurt, they made a hasty retreat out of the building. It's every man for himself in West Hall at night.

A particularly memorable incident occurred one night when every toilet in the building flushed at precisely 3:00 A.M. In paranormal circles, that time is often referred to as *dead time*, the best hour of night to make contact with the spirit world. It's also considered the *antihour*, or *Antichrist hour*. Jesus Christ is said to have died at 3:00 P.M. on Good Friday, so the opposite time, or antihour, is 3:00 A.M., which mocks the crucifixion. Hence, if paranormal incidents begin occurring at 3:00 A.M. in one's house or business, some believe it may indicate the presence of an evil spirit. Skeptics of the synchronized flushing-toilet incident at West Hall said it was merely the result of a heavy downpour overloading the city sewer system, causing the toilet water on the premises to "burp" simultaneously. Others have used scientific means to support the theory that West Hall is haunted, including recordings of electronic voice phenomena (EVPs), erratic electromagnetic field (EMF) readings, and countless photographs depicting what is thought to be spirit energy, mostly in the form of orbs. Paranormal investigators and renowned psychics, such as Lorraine Warren, have given an emphatic nod to the question of whether West Hall is haunted.

The Show Must Go On

She died in a room adorned with old photographs of herself, taken when she was in her prime. Of course, vaudeville superstar Eva Tanguay wasn't able to return to that happy time in the flesh, but with her soul no longer tethered to a physical body, has she accomplished her dream of returning to the stage? Many believe she now haunts the Cohoes Music Hall.

Tanguay's life began and ended in poverty, but from the time the former Cohoes resident first started performing at the music hall in the 1890s until 1929, she enjoyed immense wealth and fame. By the age of thirty, she was earning more than any other vaudeville performer of her time. Though her voice was mediocre, her carefree demeanor and daring songs and outfits captivated audiences everywhere, catapulting her to fame. Then at the age of fifty, it all fell apart for her. The stock market, in which Eva had invested two million dollars, suddenly crashed, and she lost everything. To make matters worse, she soon lost her health, losing her sight and becoming plagued with arthritis within two years of going broke. After twenty years of confinement and suffering in her Hollywood home, she died in 1947. The doctor who had checked in on her the night before her death told the *New York Times* that she had been in good spirits and spoke longingly "of the past in which she lived."

Built in 1874 by newspaper publisher James Maston and textile manufacturer William Acheson, the Cohoes Music Hall at 58 Remsen Street was three stories: The first floor had stores and a post office; the second floor consisted of a storage room and offices, including the ticket office; and the third floor housed the elaborate theater area and stage, which was where the magic happened, for at least a couple decades. By 1905, it became apparent that the building required extensive maintenance. Coupled with the decreased profit due to competition, the costs made it impossible to justify keeping the hall open. It was ultimately closed and remained vacant and neglected for more than sixty years. In 1969, the city purchased it for just $1 and began renovations to open it once again as a music hall. That was when the ghost sightings and strange occurrences began, as often happens during periods of remodeling.

A number of people have reported seeing a female apparition in the balcony area. Most say she strongly resembles Eva Tanguay, but others have described a female spirit in 1930s-era clothing or an angry-looking woman in a black dress. A male apparition has been seen as well, in the aisles and on stage; he announces his presence with a low, disembodied voice that has never been traced to a source. Some say he's the former stage manager who died when a sandbag fell on him many years ago. Because props that were purposely placed near the stage before shows have sometimes disappeared, being replaced by others that nobody had requested, the staff speculates that perhaps the deceased stage manager is determined to continue running the show. Why should a minor detail like one's sudden passing keep him from performing his duties?

Today, the Cohoes Music Hall is occupied by C-R Productions, Inc., a non-profit organization headed by Jim Charles and Tony Rivera whose goal, since 2002, has been to revitalize the hall by offering high-quality performances and educational programs.

Rods among the Planes in Albany

Sunday, October 20, 2002, was a day one young videographer from WXXA-TV Fox 23 in Albany would never forget. He was parked on the Troy-Schenectady Road that afternoon with the rather dull assignment of filming planes taking off from Albany International Airport when he unknowingly captured a mysterious object streaking across the sky. Things were about to get pretty intense back at the studio.

After returning to WXXA, the photographer began reviewing his footage at slow speed. Suddenly, he noticed something peculiar that he hadn't seen at the time of filming—a bizarre, rod-like object streaking through the sky above the clouds, just as Northwest Airlines Flight 1549 was taking off for Detroit. The object, which was larger and faster than any plane, stood out like a sore thumb when viewing the footage frame by frame. It was moving so fast that it was only in seven frames, according to the photographer, and its appearance on the film lasted just a quarter of a second. Yet, when played in slow motion, there was no denying its presence.

The photographer and other staff at the station made copies of the clip before officials from the Albany County Sheriff's Department, accompanied by four agents from the Albany FBI field office, appeared at the station. According to several witnesses, they viewed the footage and then "convinced" the cameraman to hand over the original tape to them. A supervisor later said that the station had willingly provided the tape to the FBI agents, because their station always cooperated with law enforcement agencies. No official determination, however, was ever released by the FBI, even after repeated status checks.

The National UFO Reporting Center (NUFORC) was contacted early the next morning by a news reporter at the television station and asked for their expertise regarding the footage. From that point on, NUFORC was continually kept apprised of events as they unfolded, and unlike some agencies, they released an extensive report regarding the entire incident. An independent forensic video analyst meticulously analyzed a copy of the tape and found the object in question to be genuine, not superimposed or retouched. According to his report, the velocity of the object in the footage was considerable and its size was immense. The analyst further determined that the object's four appendages, believed to be two sets of wings, were capsular in structure. A TSA security screener at the Albany International Airport told the press that he had seen the video and confirmed that the speeding, rod-shaped UFO had not appeared on radar.

The UFO footage was shown on the WXXA Fox 23 newscast the first evening, if only just the one time. Featured on various online sources, including *UFO Roundup*, the Fox report described the videographer's finding, saying the object was "long, slender, [and had] two sets of small wings." CNN Headline News also ran a story and the video clip on Wednesday of that week. And that was it.

Though it remained the talk of the town for some time, the Albany International Airport UFO incident was quickly hushed in the public arena. The video clip was suddenly unavailable from the news sites where it was first posted. The reason given was that overwhelming demand crashed their video servers. The footage, however, was mentioned on the History Channel documentary television series *Monster Quest*, in an episode called "Unidentified Flying Creatures" that first aired on January 9, 2008. One link that still had the video available at the time of this writing is www.roswellrods.com/albany.html. Watch it and decide for yourself if it's "just a bug" or lens reflection, as some skeptics in the YouTube community suggest.

Or could it be an authentic UFO? While you ponder that question, keep in mind that the FBI apparently has never offered an official explanation for the video anomaly.

Nun on the Run

The College of Saint Rose was founded as a Roman Catholic college for women in 1920, but today roughly forty-five hundred young men and women from diverse backgrounds grace the campus that is nestled between Western and Morris avenues in Albany. Most of the college's residence halls are located on Madison Avenue (aka U.S. Route 20 and the old Cherry Valley Turnpike), which runs straight through the campus. Whether those residence halls attract ghosts of the old turnpike, or whether the spirits are somehow associated with the college, the halls of Saint Rose are believed to be haunted by someone. Ghosts on college campuses are not unusual by any means. What is unusual and oddly endearing is the spin some Christian colleges put on paranormal activity that is reported on their campuses.

On October 18, 2006, the *Saint Rose Chronicle* ran an article, written by Ashley Melsert, about a nun who had a supernatural encounter in Carey Hall at 944 Madison Avenue. The nun was alone in the building, walking down the stairs from the second floor to the first floor, when a ball of fire materialized out of thin air and floated directly toward her. The stunned woman started backing up the stairs, keeping her eye on the fireball that was clearly following her. When she reached the second-floor landing, she turned and raced back to her room. The next day, she asked her priest what it could have been. He told her it was merely an electrical weather phenomenon known as "St. Elmo's Fire," and that it was named for St. Erasmus of Formiae, the patron saint of sailors, because seamen often saw the strange lights on their ships during thunderstorms at sea. The problem is that the phenomenon requires a high amount of electrical voltage, like that released during a lightning storm, and it doesn't consciously follow people up stairways. Nevertheless, priests are supposed to bring comfort, not fear, and in this case, the priest's theory certainly calmed the nun, especially when he told her that it was a sign from St. Elmo himself that she was destined to do something of great importance.

Incoming freshmen at Saint Rose are often briefed on the campus's alleged ghost stories to prepare them for their own chance encounters, and the number of stories to pass along is growing. Besides the nun's run-in with the fireball in Carey, there was a young man whose suitcase kept emptying itself; the clothes tossed about as he attempted to pack. It happened each time he tried to leave the room, as if some unseen entity was trying to keep him from leaving or just trying to annoy him. There was also a skeptical resident assistant who was casually telling one of her charges a ghost story associated with Carey Hall, when a nearby window shade suddenly flew up, causing her to rethink her cynicism.

A playful child ghost causes mischief in Quillian Hall at 953 Madison Avenue. She allegedly died in a fire there, and students can point to charred wood in a renovated staircase to add substance to that detail. The child ghost locks students out of their rooms and awakens them at night, asking them to play with her. Some students hear the sound of someone playing jacks on the floor, although the pieces of the game can't be found.

Morris Hall is haunted by a priest whose apparition has been spotted by several people—sometimes in reflective surfaces and sometimes in the location of the former chapel altar from when the building was a convent. Students have seen items fly off the windowsills and heard the faint sound of flute music. One girl was awakened at exactly 3:00 A.M. by the rattling of the mirror on the back of her door. A male student once watched as footprints pressed into his bedding, and it looked like someone was walking all around him on his bed. Now that's a hard one to spin!

Gateway to Hell

Forest Park Cemetery on Pinewoods Avenue in Brunswick is an abandoned cemetery that is as famous for its alleged paranormal activity as it is for its urban legends. Established in 1897 by a group of Troy businessmen, it was expected to be a two-hundred-acre, garden-variety cemetery with rolling hills, beautiful landscaping, and wooded trails. Because of poor budgeting, however, the Forest Park Cemetery Corporation went bankrupt in 1914, leaving only one-tenth of the property developed as a cemetery. The remaining land was sold to the adjacent Country Club of Troy. In 1918, some out-of-town investors purchased and reincorporated the cemetery, calling it Forest Hills. More than a thousand interments were not enough to save the second corporation from bankruptcy in the 1930s. The cemetery seemed destined to be abandoned yet again. In 1990, New York State municipal laws mandated that the town of Brunswick assume responsibility for the cemetery; and today, the Forest Park Cemetery Advisory Council is tasked with restoring and maintaining the ill-fated grounds. With the exception of its stint as Forest Hills Cemetery, the graveyard has retained its original, proper name to this day, although some call it Pinewoods Cemetery for its location on that avenue. Still others call it the Gateway to Hell.

The urban legends associated with Forest Park Cemetery, perpetuated by the news media, have in part earned it the title of "most haunted" cemetery in the state. The Hudson Valley is one of many places where a young female hitchhiker is said to catch a ride home at night; then, as the driver passes by a cemetery, he looks over to find that she has vanished from the moving vehicle with nary a door having been opened. That's what a cab driver said happened to him on Pinewood Avenue, according to a 1996 Troy *Record* article. There is also the familiar legend of a young couple in the 1940s or 1950s who parked in the quiet, deserted graveyard one night, but were interrupted by a strange sound. The man got out of the car to check it out and seconds later, a scraping sound was heard on the roof of the car. The lady then got out and was horrified to find her boyfriend dangling from the tree that just happened to have a sturdy limb hanging smack over the roof of the car. Such are the urban legends we hear at slumber parties, personalized to our own locations.

Forest Park is sometimes called the Gateway to Hell for another reason: It now looks the part thanks to vandalism. Statues of angels are missing their heads and limbs and tombstones have been knocked over and broken. Mother Nature has also had a hand in the cemetery's decay, because a type of moss that turns red when rubbed in humid weather grows on some of the monuments; hence, the "bleeding statues" reports.

Then there are the other reports. People hear babies crying. Others see a large, threatening apparition that seems to be guarding the remains of the receiving tomb. As people approach, the spirit leaps toward the woods in a single bound. Investigators have captured some of these strange occurrences on film, audio, and various detection devices.

Central New York's IMOVES has visited the cemetery several times, capturing orbs and apparitions on film, video footage of white floating images coming from behind the receiving tomb toward the cameraman, and erratic readings on energy detection equipment right before their batteries died. In October 2008, John Gray and Bob Donnelly of the Troy *Record* visited the cemetery with psychic Ann Fisher. Although Bob, the photographer, was using fresh batteries, the first set drained quickly while he aimed the camera in whatever direction the psychic sensed a presence. He replaced the dead set with another new set, but those, too, died within thirty seconds.

Ghostly Chatterbox

When members of the Northern New York Paranormal Research Society (NNYPRS) investigated the Irish Mist Restaurant in Troy in October 2008, they left with enough personal experiences and paranormal evidence to conclude that the location "may be experiencing both residual and true hauntings," according to society founder Merrill McKee. The most convincing incident occurred when one of the seven investigators present that night came face-to-face with a full-bodied apparition (FBA). Approximately two feet in front of him, a bald elderly man wearing a navy blue shirt appeared, standing sideways and looking in another direction, seemingly unaware of the presence of the investigator. The apparition appeared to be solid, instead of fuzzy and colorless like many that have been reported. But the image only lasted a few seconds, barely enough time for the investigator to process what he was witnessing, before it dissolved into thin air.

The four-story building at 285 2nd Street in Troy was erected in 1846 for the city's second-oldest stove foundry, Empire Stove Works, originally called the Anson Atwood Company. Empire was also the second-largest cast-iron stove manufacturer in the Northeast at that time, employing two hundred men and boys and producing roughly ten thousand stoves during an era when Troy was recognized worldwide as a stove-producing city. But it was just one of several such companies in the city competing for the local, national, and world market of cooking and heating stoves, as well as train car wheels. Though the stove plant had become idle by the turn of the century, a building beside it housing the Hislop Scale Works caught fire on January 28, 1902, when "a spark from an emery wheel in the japanning department landed in a barrel of gasoline, which exploded and spread the flames in every direction," according to the Troy *Record*. Panic ensued, and Hislop workers "fled for their lives," leaving their tools and overcoats behind. Miraculously, there were no casualties; but the fire spread to Empire, then owned by George W. Swett. The *Record* said, "The plant is practically destroyed, although the walls remain standing." The scorched building remained vacant until 1920, when Lindy's Hardware moved in. Lindy's occupied the building for nearly seventy-nine years, until the late president and owner, Millard Elliott Rosenthal, retired in 1999. Though Rosenthal is gone, the large, painted Lindy's sign on the side of the building provides a constant reminder of the man and his business.

In 2001, Donald Russell and Tony Zartman opened the building as the Irish Mist Restaurant, which included a bar and banquet facility. Since its opening, employees have reported feeling a light touch when nobody is around them, according to the NNYPRS post-investigative report. Many have said they often feel as if they're not alone when they're the only ones there. One individual told the investigators about the time he was setting up after hours for the next day's banquet. He had placed tablecloths neatly on the tables before leaving to grab the glassware. When he returned moments later, a tablecloth had been completely pulled off one of the tables; the same thing happened several more times that night. Another incident reported to NNYPRS occurred when a sound crew was filming a movie on the fourth floor of the old building. They set up their equipment for a sound check and then everyone left the floor. When they returned, a twenty-three-minute recording of "ghostly conversation" awaited them. The spirits of the Irish Mist are apparently quite the little chatterboxes.

Merrill and his crew added their own experiences to the growing list of alleged paranormal incidents. Besides the full-bodied apparition, one member told of a distinct feeling of being watched, just as the employees had described. Unexplainable shadows seen by several investigators on the second floor could not be duplicated or debunked. When two investigators were on the second floor, they saw metal rods that had been leaning on a chair across the room crash to the floor for no apparent reason. Besides these personal experiences, anomalous photographs and video footage revealed possible spirit energy in various forms, and a few audio clips with "questionable sounds" were acquired.

Trapped in Paradise

Today, Union College students strolling through America's oldest manmade campus garden find the eight manicured acres to be a delightful, peaceful sanctuary, a welcome respite from their hectic academic schedules. But long ago this spot bore witness to a singular, godless act of cruelty that snuffed out the life of a beautiful young woman. Her agonized screams punctuated the stillness for what had to seem like an eternity, and although the ashes of her remains have long since been carried away by the wind and the elements, her spirit seems trapped in the paradise that is Jackson's Garden.

This is a story familiar to those who have been to Union College, to the residents of Schenectady, and to horticulture enthusiasts. Isaac Wilbur Jackson graduated from the private liberal arts school in 1826 and remained associated with it for the rest of his life, teaching math, philosophy, optics, astronomy, electricity, and acoustics there. In 1831, Jackson was asked by college president Eliphalet Nott to plant a formal garden on the property, an idea the president had envisioned when the campus was still being designed. Jackson proved to be such a skilled and gifted gardener that he became the Superintendent of the College Garden, spending forty-six years tweaking his masterpiece. But there were others who had strong ties to the land. When Jackson died in 1877, his daughter, Julia Jackson Benedict, took over the garden and proved to be a chip off the old block. Under her supervision, the garden grew larger and lusher every year. Another Union graduate, John C. Van Voast, assumed the responsibility of tending Jackson's garden for many decades, beginning in 1887. Then the wife of college president, Dixon Ryan Fox, accepted responsibility for overseeing maintenance of the garden from 1935 to 1945. After that, the college took on the task, using both hired landscapers and volunteer gardeners to keep the garden paradise groomed. Among the number of people with ties to the garden, Alice Vander Veer's name tops the list.

Vander Veer, a name used by one of the earliest Dutch settlers of Long Island, means "from the ferry." Cornelise Janse Vander Veer, who emigrated from Holland in 1659, was first to use the name in New Amsterdam (later New York City). In 1672, it is said that a young woman named Alice Vander Veer was tied to either a stake or a pine tree and burned to death on the property now known as Jackson's Garden. She had fallen in love with a man her father did not approve of, so her father killed the young man. An angry mob avenged their friend's death by allegedly killing Alice in a misguided attempt to make her father feel the sorrow they felt at the senseless loss of a loved one. That's one version of the story. The other version has both father and daughter burned at the stake. Regardless of the details, many people now claim that Jackson's Garden is haunted by Alice. They say that on the first full moon of a summer night, Alice's apparition can be seen floating toward the garden, as if helplessly repeating her lonely death march.

According to Union College's newsletter, *Chronicle*, of October 31, 2003, the ghost in the garden really created a buzz on the first full moon of summer that year. On July 14, the college hosted a national conference with about 150 annual fund officers, and most of them were housed in Davidson Hall. That night, there was a campus-wide power failure; when it had not been restored by morning, the visitors had to be transferred to a local hotel. The campus safety officer suggested that perhaps it was the work of Alice.

Valley of Peace

O vale of peace! O haunt serene!
O hill encircled shades!
No footsteps rude, or fiery neigh
Of iron steed o'er graded way,
Your Sylvan steep invades

In the verse above, American poet Lydia Sigourney (1791–1865) was referring to the town of Schaghticoke, and more specifically to the Knickerbocker Mansion, when she wrote "Valley of Peace" after visiting in the nineteenth century. The red-and-green homestead at 132 Knickerbocker Road was built in 1770 by Johannes Knickerbocker, great-grandson of Dutch colonist Harmen Jansen van Wyhe, who arrived in America in 1674. Washington Irving made the name famous when he took the pen name "Diedrich Knickerbocker" in his 1809 satire *History of New York*, after befriending Johannes Knickerbocker's son, Herman, and spending much time at the Knickerbocker Mansion. Herman, a famous lawyer, congressman, and assemblyman, was known as "the Prince of Schaghticoke," because of his old-fashioned hospitality and bigheartedness. But he was also known as a bit of a practical joker, according to a 2004 *New York Times* article.

For 250 years, the Knickerbockers traveled the dirt road leading to their isolated estate. Today, the landscape hasn't changed much. There's but one farmhouse across the road and then nothing for at least a mile. Just past the mansion, behind a stone wall, is the Knickerbocker family cemetery, which is open to the public. You can see how such a setting—the remote location and sheer age of the weathered structure—could lead to rumors of the mansion being haunted. One resident who grew up nearby said that the roof caved in and the front wall crumbled before the historical society began restoration. Neighborhood kids, well aware of the ghost stories that had been circulating for years, bragged of trespassing on the property, and vandalism reared its ugly head.

One tour guide fervently believes the home is haunted and refuses to go inside after dark. Photographs taken inside, especially in the attic area, often reveal multiple orbs. Maybe it's Herman, the prankster, or a former slave who is unwilling to leave. According to the December 1876 issue of *Harper's New Monthly Magazine*, the Knickerbockers' slave quarters in the winter months were in the cellar, where the help warmed themselves by a huge fireplace. Often, they sat telling "unearthly tales of ghosts and goblins." And even though the slaves in New York State were emancipated in 1824, the article said, "many of them remained at the old homestead until death removed them from it; their attachment to home and to the members of the family remaining undiminished to the last moment." The slaves of the family were obviously very fond of the Knickerbockers and the life they enjoyed on the estate, and such a strong attachment to a person or place is said to motivate hauntings.

Today, the Knickerbocker Historical Society is restoring the mansion, which was added to the National Register of Historic Places in 1972. A new roof has been put on the house and a collapsed wall was repaired. The current fund-raising efforts will go toward restoring the interior and replacing the windows. In October, the mansion hosts Halloween events, which include telling stories about the reported ghosts of the mansion.

Tossed About by Spooks

Passing by the site of the old Aged Men Philanthropic Asylum in 1892, author and famed horticulturist Louis Menand, for whom the village of Menands is named, recalled his five-year stint in the building now known as Menands Manor, where he lived with his wife half a century earlier. In the book he was writing at the time, *Autobiography and Recollections of Incidents Connected with Horticulture Affairs, Etc.*, he included an appendix in which he speaks of the house being haunted since the 1840s.

Today's tenant, the Council of Community Services of New York State, has a staff of two dozen, and virtually all of them say they have experienced something of a paranormal nature. In fact, the employees are so accustomed to the unexplainable incidents they have witnessed that they openly share their experiences with the news media and the general public. In 2007, the organization hosted "A Benefit Evening at the Haunted Menands Manor" that included a tour of the premises, as well as discussions with former tenants, the town historian, and the current occupants regarding their supernatural experiences in the building.

The friendly little community of Menands is located in the town of Colonie, just north of Albany on the Hudson River. In the late 1790s, according to Colonie historian Kevin Franklin, a prominent Albany soap manufacturer named Joseph Strain built the original part of the Menands Manor on the Albany and Troy Road in Watervliet (now 272 Broadway in Menands). The site is now listed in both the state's historic register and the National Register of Historic Places. Louis Menand rented the place from 1842 until 1847, later writing about his time in what was already widely believed to be the haunted house of the community, though he steadfastly scoffed at the notion. He wrote in his 1892 autobiography:

We hardly were moved in than some of the few and far apart neighbors informed me that they were surprised that I had hired the place for such a long lease; that nobody could live in it but for a short time, on account of the aforesaid progenies of the devil. Rather weak minds, or something equal to it.

When the wet nurse hired by the Menands to nourish their new-born daughter was assailed by a powerful ghost at the foot of Mrs. Menand's bed one night, Louis dismissed the experience as fabricated and was even concerned that such imaginings might be "infused" into the blood of the child she nursed. "A mass of inflated flesh was uncongenial to the nutrition of a weak, delicate child materially speaking," he quipped, adding, "and then probably worse mentally speaking, nursed up by a mind haunted by the existence of ghosts, of spooks impalpable, intangible things infusing her blood in the system of a frail being, it was unnatural, monstrous!" Suffice it to say that Menand was no fan of ghost stories . . . or of breast-feeding, for that matter. Recounting the poor nurse's paranormal experience in the house, he wrote:

> We had to get a nurse; a large, stout, immense woman, whom from the appearance one could have supposed she could nurse up half a dozen. . . . She slept in the same room with my wife on a cot at the foot of my wife's bed. One morning early I went in the room to see how they were all . . . when in a great excitement—a flurry—[the nurse] said that she would not sleep in that house another night for anything in the world, that the greatest part of the night she had been tossed, or rather heaved up, as if by the swelling of waves under the cot-bed. . . . from that time, she never came anymore in the house but in day time, but she never neglected to divulge the incident of having been tossed by spooks, and everybody believed the story, as she did herself, [but] wondered how it was that neither of us four in the house did not hear anything.

Although Menand did not believe the house was haunted, others in the community did. So as the expiration of Menand's lease approached in 1847, he should not have been surprised that two men interested in buying the property were curious about the rumors. To one from Albany who asked him sheepishly about the stories he'd heard, Menand impatiently responded, "Is it possible, sir, that an intelligent man as you seem to be should believe in such stupidities?" After that man departed "in a very bad humor," another came along, and when the line of questioning turned to spooks, Menand recalled that the man "did not listen to my jestings as patiently as the former, and he abruptly made his exit; from a few words he was grumbling as he walked away, I supposed he did not like my sarcasms." When Menand's landlord found out he had ridiculed the two potential buyers for believing such nonsense, he was understandably not pleased. Menand said the landlord was punishing him for his "trifling with hobgoblins and for the credulity of those believing in them."

As it turned out, when the lease expired and the Menands moved out, the owner's daughter got married and moved in. When her husband stopped by Menand's horticulture business to pick up some shrubs, he told Menand that if there were any ghosts, he would take care of it: "I will fix them alright; if any, they must be in the crevices of the old walls, and I will paper them all over and fumigate the whole building from cellar to garret." Apparently, that method of exorcising the spirits was ineffective.

Sometime in the mid-1800s, the house was sold to the Perry family; and in 1877, Mrs. Perry sold the large lot and house to the Home for Aged Men, a corporation created to accommodate needy males of at least sixty-five years of age, especially Civil War veterans. The corporation added two large wings on the structure and made the necessary alterations to accommodate seventy-five men before opening for business a year after the purchase. By 1925, it became necessary to further expand the building for even more men and provide them with an infirmary and two sunrooms. After Social Security was implemented by Franklin D. Roosevelt in the 1930s in response to the Great Depression, the home saw a steady decline in residential applications. In 1975, because of the decrease in revenue, women were finally allowed in. Still, the resident numbers declined to the point that the Home for Aged Men and Women was no longer fiscally viable. It closed in the 1980s, only to be reopened and renovated by the Center for the Disabled in the mid-1990s. The Council of Community Services purchased the property in 2002.

The ongoing paranormal activity at Menands Manor runs the gamut from seeing shadows to undoing the handiwork of hired electricians, according to James V. Franco in the July 2008 article "What is Haunting Menands Manor?" in the Troy *Record*. Executive Director Doug Sauer was interviewed for the piece, and he told Franco that he has seen shadows go past doorways and heard doors opening and closing. Other employees interviewed have experienced electronic equipment malfunctions, cold spots, and unexplainable sounds. Some have seen small objects fly through the air. Contractors working on the electric returned to the site one day to find that during the night someone had undone all their work.

One employee responded to an alarm at the house with her sister. They made a hasty departure shortly after hearing something heavy "like a metal bed" being pulled across the floor upstairs. (Perhaps this was the same spirit who violently shook the cot Menand's nurse was lying on in the 1840s.) The two had arrived armed with a video recorder, determined to catch something on camera, because the alarm is always going off mysteriously; so they were recording during the time they were in the building. When they played back the footage, according to Franco, everything from the moment after they entered until the moment before they left was missing.

Fire in the Library!

On March 29, 1911, the San Antonio *Light* in Texas reported on a fire that occurred two days earlier in Albany, the capital of New York: "While the fire was at its height, four men were reported missing," the paper said. "One of them, Samuel Abbott, night watchman in the state library, is still missing and is believed to have been burned to death. His body is probably buried beneath the mass of debris."

The devastating fire had in fact struck the State Capitol itself, destroying much of the western side, including the State Library and many of its countless historic books and documents. Around 2:30 A.M., Abbott raced down the third-floor corridor screaming, "There's a fire in the Assembly Library!" In his efforts to ensure that everyone else escaped the burning building, he sealed his own fate. His body, charred beyond recognition, was later found in the southwest corner of the building on the fourth floor, where the flames raged the fiercest. The only clue to his identity was his watch. It was speculated at the time that Abbott died attempting to dutifully rescue some of the state's most valuable relics and double-check every room to make sure everyone was out. But at some point during the smoky chaos, he became trapped. Many believe his spirit has remained trapped ever since as well.

The capitol, sitting majestically on top of a hill in Capitol Park, was the most expensive government building of its kind when it was constructed in 1899. It was an architectural marvel that was deemed "absolutely fireproof," according to news sources of the time, so there was no fire insurance on the building or its priceless contents, including original Dutch and English colonial records. There was only one fire alarm, and because of that, the night watchman either lost his life attempting to reach it or attempting to save people and valuable relics. No definitive cause was ever found for the tragic fire, but the theories suggest that either a cigarette was carelessly tossed in a wastebasket at a clerk's desk in the assembly library or the fuse of an electric push button became electrified, causing the fateful spark. Of all the places for the fire to start, the library, with its three-quarters of a million books and original manuscripts, had to be the worst.

Though some have dubbed the Capitol ghost "George the Janitor," it's more likely that the classic janitorial sounds of keys jangling, doors closing, and footsteps going up and down the corridors at all hours of the night are instead those of Samuel, the night watchman. The unexplainable shadows seen and voices heard by employees working the night shift could be attributed to anyone who is no longer among the living, including George, if there indeed was such a janitor. But if a grayish blur races toward you, and you simultaneously feel an icy chill pass right through your body, chances are you got in the way of a night watchman on his mission to save people and priceless state property in a burning building. That's what happened to one employee, right before a nearby coworker experienced a Marilyn Monroe wardrobe malfunction when her skirt flew up in the breeze caused by the passing spirit. Though several psychics have attempted to release the ghost of the Capitol, their efforts have not yet been entirely successful. Paranormal activity continues to this day, according to some who work there. Until someone is successful in relieving the poor man of his duty, Samuel Abbott's ghost may be destined to replicate both his routine nightly rounds and his last frantic moments.

The Coffee Jitters

It's rather ironic that a popular Albany coffee sanctuary was once a residence with a dangerous drug lab in its basement. When the lab at 217 Wolf Road was raided by law enforcement authorities in the early 1980s, the only casualty was said to be a dog that was killed accidentally. Customers and employees of Professor Java's Coffee Sanctuary have heard the hapless pooch bark since the first day of business, and employees feel the basement still has a feeling of eeriness about it, causing some of them to think twice about going down there when the need arises. Manager Charles Pemburn said, "To be honest, it has been fun to watch [people] run outside in search of a barking dog, only to realize that the sound grows quieter as you leave the building. The barking came from within the sanctuary walls." While the pup seems to be moving on, as indicated by the steadily decreasing reports of phantom barking, other spooks have done an admirable job filling the void.

According to Pemburn, Frank Figliomeni purchased the house in the mid-1990s to accommodate his "vision to create a café that would serve the community by providing great service, freshly roasted coffee, and a perfect, relaxed atmosphere." Figliomeni had heard rumors that the place was haunted, but didn't buy into them until his own close encounter with a male apparition. He was washing his hands in the men's room when he glanced up in the mirror to see a man standing behind him. The spirit looked to be in his fifties and was wearing a suit from the 1920s. In the split second it took for the owner to spin around and face the intruder, the man vanished.

Others have seen a similar apparition wearing an old-time trench coat. It enters the building and heads directly to the library, but is nowhere to be found by anyone who follows him. Whatever existed on the property before the current structure was built in the 1940s may be responsible for the appearance of the man, as well as the spirits of a woman and a youngster reported by employees and customers. Figliomeni has seen an apparition of a boy about ten years old, and he's heard its laughter, even at 6 A.M. when nobody but the owner is in the building. Others have heard the boy spirit running around the building, and he has been blamed for playfully moving furniture after hours. A female apparition with long hair has been seen walking into the back room, where she vanishes into thin air, like the gentleman with the trench coat.

Besides the apparitions, Professor Java's Coffee Sanctuary experiences an abundance of other paranormal activity: dishes rattling, appliances going on and off on their own, and pictures falling off the walls. Yet, even with these occasional incidents, the café lives up to its name as a haven where one can escape the daily hustle and bustle and relax with a cup of java. If there are spirits stopping by now and then, they do not feel in any way threatening. To the contrary, the owner says, they seem very pleasant.

Bragging Rights

When the state capital's tour of haunted sites begins in the main parlor of your building and you host an event called "Ten Broeck Uncorked: The Ghosts of Ten Broeck," you must have something to brag about. Apparently, the Albany County Historical Association (ACHA) does. The society owns, operates, and houses their headquarters in the house-museum known as the Ten Broeck Mansion at 9 Ten Broeck Place in Albany.

Abraham Ten Broeck, who built the mansion in 1797, was one of the city's wealthiest businessmen, primarily because of his booming lumber business. Beginning in 1775, he never slowed down, first serving as a delegate to the Second Continental Congress and then heroically commanding the New York Militia at the Battle of Saratoga. He served as the mayor of Albany, a state senator, a judge, the president of the Bank of Albany, a trustee of Union College, and the president of the Albany Public Library. In the midst of all this, he had a Federal-style house built, complete with manicured lawns and lush gardens, in what was then called the Township of Watervliet. He named his refuge Prospect. By that time, however, the youngest of his and wife Elizabeth's five children was eighteen, and the prominent couple was getting on in years. They would only enjoy Prospect for twelve years, before Abraham died at the age of sixty-seven on January 19, 1810, and Elizabeth died in 1813, both right there in their mansion.

The house was transformed in the Greek Revival style and purchased by Thomas Worth Olcott in 1848. The Olcott family renamed it Arbor Hill, and today the entire area in which Ten Broeck Mansion sits is called the Arbor Hill neighborhood. One hundred years after the Olcott family moved into Ten Broeck Mansion, the heirs of Robert Olcott donated the mansion to the Albany County Historical Association, and ever since, it has been rumored to be haunted.

Psychic Ann Fisher sensed the spirit of Abraham Ten Broeck and told the *Times Union* that he "doesn't want to leave." The executive director of Ten Broeck, Brian Buff, admits that he has seen things that have left him baffled, like large objects being moved during the night when he was the last person out. For example, a chair in the upstairs hallway is kept precisely parked on a rug in front of a closet door, but some mornings, Buff has found the chair pulled away from the door, as if someone tried to get into (or out of) the closet during the night. Buff stops short of saying the place is definitely haunted, but he's not the only person to have experienced something unexplainable. Others have reported seeing a mysterious soldier wearing a War of 1812 uniform, as well as young females descending the staircase from the third floor to the second floor.

While the primary purpose of the non-profit, state-chartered ACHA is to preserve and explain the history of Albany, its staff is wise enough to realize the benefits of admitting that there may be some interactive artifacts of a ghostly nature that are not always on display. The museum is open from April through December, Wednesdays through Sundays, and is closed on holidays.

Mid-
Hudson Valley

THE MID-HUDSON REGION CONSISTS OF FIVE COUNTIES: DUTCHESS, Orange, Ulster, Columbia, and Greene. This region's haunted properties include some of the great estates, such as Lindenwald, the home of President Martin Van Buren; the 1841 Goshen Courthouse, where a spirit's skull is embedded in mortar over the entrance; and two churches, one of which houses a homicidal hobgoblin. The ghost-infested Shanley Hotel in Napanoch, with its guaranteed paranormal activity and endless supply of credible evidence, is a must-see for ghost enthusiasts. The spirits there are a dime a dozen, as are the UFOs over Pine Bush, an area considered to be a popular hotspot for sightings. There have also been several Bigfoot sightings in this region, including one that resulted in the sensational "Baby Bigfoot" footage.

Claudius Smith's Cranium

Claudius Smith was defiant to the end, and he continues his insolence even in death, haunting those who walk under him. That's right—under him! His skull is embedded in the wall above the door of the 1841 Goshen Courthouse, thanks to a mason who allegedly filled the infamous cranium with mortar and cemented it to the wall during construction with all the reverence Smith was due.

Known as the "Scourge of the Highlands," Smith and his gang, including his sons, were the worst outlaws in the area; they robbed, murdered, and terrorized wealthy patriot settlers throughout Goshen and the entire Hudson Highlands region. The "Cow-boys," as they were called, were sympathetic to the British cause, according to an 1879 *New York Times* article.

> The public road from New York passed along the Ramapo River at the base of the Highlands, and at the time, the headquarters of the American Army were in the Highlands, quantities of supplies and arms were carried in wagons along this road. Frequent raids were made upon these wagons by the Cow-boys, who killed or put the guards to flight, and carried off to their dens in the mountains much valuable booty. Wealthy families were robbed of their plate, and frequently large amounts of money; horses and cattle were stolen and sent to the British lines in droves. Resistance on the part of any resident whose house was visited by these marauders cost him his life, and willful and unprovoked murders were common.

Nobody knew where or when Smith would strike next, because his followers at least knew how to keep a secret; they were adept at hiding in a network of caves they had claimed as their storehouses, so it was difficult to organize any kind of united effort to locate the fearsome posse. The straw that broke the camel's back was the murder of Maj. Nathaniel Strong of Blooming Grove, and a reward was finally offered for Smith's capture. He was subsequently tracked to Long Island and sent back to Goshen, where he was tried, convicted, and sentenced to be hanged on January 22, 1779. The *New York Times*, one hundred years after the fact, described the hanging as follows:

> On the morning of the hanging, the Courthouse square was packed with people who had come from many miles around to see the dreaded scourge of the Highlands die. . . . Claudius Smith was arrayed in a fine broadcloth suit with massive silver buttons on his coat and large gold buckles on his shoes. As he passed through the crowd, he nodded to acquaintances that he saw. . . . The rope was then adjusted around the necks of the three men, and the cart was driven from under them. Dolson and Delamer struggled terribly; but Smith, evidently determined to show no feeling, hung straight from the rope, and scarcely a shudder passed over his gigantic

frame, although life was not extinct until long after his companions were dead. Smith's body was buried on the spot where the gallows stood, which is now in the public park of Goshen, near the main street. His bones have never been disturbed.

His bones have never been disturbed! Ah, but they had been, less than four decades before that statement was made in the news article. During construction of the 1841 Goshen Courthouse at 101 Main Street near the same grounds on which Smith was hanged and buried, workmen dug up a pine box with a skeleton believed to be Smith's, because he had uncommonly long femur bones and a large frame. A local farmer took the thigh bone and had a knife handle fashioned out of it, and the skull was kept on display at a local meat market until the courthouse was near completion. Then a mason allegedly took the skull and inserted it into the mortar above the entrance of the courthouse. Ever since then, there have been reports of strange rapping sounds coming from within the walls of the Greek Revival–style courthouse and orbs of light seen through the windows by passersby late at night. The courthouse functioned as such until 1970. Today it is home to the Orange County Genealogical Society.

Smith is also said to haunt one of his hideouts called "Claudius Smith's Den" in Harriman State Park. Unexplained lights have been seen at night in the woods surrounding the cave, and orbs have been reported flitting about in the darkness of the den, prompting some to believe that Smith and his loyal bandits continue, even in spirit, to secret themselves there. One boy in the late 1800s claimed that he peered into the cave and saw skeletal figures prodding the cave walls with sticks as if in search of the hidden treasure long rumored to be buried there. Scared senseless, he never returned to the area again. Leave it to Claudius Smith to continue his reign of terror even after his earthly days have ceased.

Little Lillian's Sad Plight

The Bardavon 1869 Opera House on Market Street in Poughkeepsie is the oldest continuously operating theater in New York State. It was built on land first used for a thriving lumber and coal business owned by one of Poughkeepsie's wealthiest men of the period,

James Collingwood. When it opened as the Collingwood Opera House in 1869, it brought in such famous performers as Edwin Booth and General Tom Thumb to perform on its magnificent stage. To keep up with the times, the opera house underwent a transformation in 1923, changing its name to the Bardavon and updating the site to accommodate vaudeville and silent films and later talking films. The roster of celebrities that the Bardavon has seen over the years is too long for this book, but a smattering of the names includes Harry Houdini, Helen Hayes, Frank Sinatra, Milton Berle, Gregg Allman, David Crosby, Ernest Borgnine, Natalie Cole, Cher, and Joan Baez.

Like most old theaters, the Bardavon may be haunted, according to Executive Director Chris Silva when interviewed for a "Hudson Valley Hauntings" piece by *Poughkeepsie Journal* reporter Alice Hunt. A ghost dubbed "Roger" is said to have been a former stage manager who was fatally shot on the premises in the late 1800s, but I could find no record of such an incident. Still, the Bardavon's technical/lighting director, Jason Adams, told me that Roger gets blamed for all things unexplainable at the opera house—water faucets turning on, lights going on and off without anyone touching the switches, and so on. It's just Roger.

But is it? Another spirit believed to haunt the building is an unidentified little girl thought to have died in a coal trolley accident when the property was still Collingwood's coal yard. Again, I could find no documentation of a fatal accident involving a young girl in newspapers from that time. I do think I discovered who the girl spirit may be, however. On March 19, 1895, the *New York Times* ran a story called "The Sad Plight of Youthful Actress," which described the tragic ordeal of nine-year-old Lillian Graham:

> The little girl was a member of "Uncle Tom's Cabin" troupe which appeared at the [Bardavon Opera House] on Saturday. She played the part of Little Eva. Saturday morning she was discovered to be ill, and the manager of the company took her to Vassar Hospital and tried to secure her admission there, but was refused, as it is only an emergency hospital and not equipped for treatment of infectious diseases. He then endeavored to have her cared for in a private house, but failed.

From there, the situation deteriorated rapidly. The local health officer ordered the sick child to the city pesthouse, a fate perhaps worse than death. It was supposed to be a shelter for infectious patients, but in reality, it only served to hasten their demise. The pesthouse was half a mile from any road in the middle of an open field. A tiny shack with a damp, uncarpeted dirt floor and one small stove to provide heat, it offered no such amenities as water or sewer. The bedding and nightclothes of previous patients were rarely cleaned before the next unfortunate patient arrived. A young nurse from the same troupe that Lillian belonged to was the only person allowed to accompany the orphan child to the pesthouse, so the two were sent off in a horse-drawn carriage.

> On their arrival . . . the nurse and her little charge got out of the carriage and found the building locked. They waited in the cold for someone to come and, after an interval, were noticed by the Superintendent of the Poor who sent one of his keepers to inquire what the trouble was. When he learned the situation, he directed his men to break the door in and build a fire and care for the ill and half-frozen little girl . . . the two were given such shelter as a half-rotten building, which had been unused for six months and was damp and cheerless . . . the little girl was put to bed in bed-clothes that have been in the pesthouse a long while and have been used by people afflicted with all sorts of diseases. The last case there was one of scarlet fever, which resulted fatally, and the bedclothes used by that patient were given to Lillian Graham.

When the city's Dr. Porteous heard of Lillian's plight, he offered to take her into his home to be nursed by his daughter, but the Board of Health told him he would have to quarantine his house, where his business was also located. So Lillian remained at the pesthouse to die, even as a member of the Board of Health called the pesthouse "a disgrace." One week after the *Times'* first article, they reported that Lillian was "suffering from diphtheria [and] is very weak, and her chances of recovery are very poor." Her father, who had divorced her dying mother several years before and lost track of both of them, read about her situation in the newspaper and came to see her, but the same heartless health officer that had sent her to the pesthouse in the first place refused to let the father (or anyone) visit her.

Jason Adams told me that the girl ghost was believed to be about eight years old, according to witnesses, and was wearing a pink, frilly southern dress. He admitted he may have "caught a glimpse" of her himself walking along the balcony landing one night as he worked alone, but he couldn't be sure. Nobody at the Bardavon was aware of the story about Lillian Graham until I wrote this piece, yet Jason's description of the apparition matches a sketch of Lillian in the March 31, 1895, edition of the *New York Times*. That was the last that any mention was made of Lillian in the paper.

Could it be that death was Lillian's only means of escaping the hellhole that was the city pesthouse? And if you had been snatched from a building that cost $50,000 to build and left at a barren shack that cost merely $200 in comparison, wouldn't you return to the former as soon as possible? If anyone haunts the Bardavon 1869 Opera House, it should be that poor little angel.

Holy Spirits

You'd be surprised how many clergymen have had encounters of the supernatural kind and how many churches have experienced highly publicized hauntings. Take the century-old Christ Church on the corner of Academy and Barclay streets in Poughkeepsie. There, the congregation and staff have experienced unexplainable incidents for more than fifty years. When the new church was built in 1888 on the southwest portion of the English Burying Ground, several dozen graves were disturbed, and the stones were relocated, fifteen of which were "securely stored" in the cellar of the church, according to J.W. Poucher's 1924 *Old Gravestones of Dutchess County, New York*.

The controversial, wildly popular Bishop James Pike served as rector for a stint in the late 1940s before moving on to much bigger things. History will remember him as a spiritual icon who helped pave the way for the Episcopal Church of the future.

Pike was an admitted believer in the supernatural and was the first person to say he had seen a ghost at Christ Church. He felt the spirit was Dr. Alexander Griswold Cummins Jr., a former rector who died on September 30, 1946, at the age of seventy-seven. Cummins had been rector since 1900 and was as outspokenly traditional as Pike was radically unconventional. Pike was sure he had seen

Cummins's ghost walking up the stairs and puttering around near the altar. He had also been attacked by a bat at the altar during mass one day just as he lit a holy candle. The entire congregation, always a full house while Pike was rector, watched as a gust of wind blew the candle out right when the bat appeared, according to Susan Smitten in *Ghosts Stories of New York State*. Those who knew Dr. Cummins say he was not a fan of candles and often blew them out quickly during his own services.

Pike died in 1969, after a tragic fall in the Judean Desert. For a twenty-year period following his death, all was quiet at the church, meaning there were no candle-snuffing incidents, no close encounters with apparitions, and no vanishing bat tricks. If Cummins had been haunting Christ Church, he took a twenty-year break following Pike's untimely death. Then in the 1990s, reports of paranormal activity began again. Bats were sometimes seen, which isn't alarming in and of itself, but the fact that the bats reportedly vanished in midair is rather odd. Candle flames in the church library, formerly the rector's office, have been snuffed out by unseen hands, again leading to speculation that Cummins had returned from the beyond. The room also became infused with a persistent icy chill, indicating that Cummins, or someone, is refusing to budge.

In the early 1900s, an elderly woman allegedly died during mass, and there are reports that her spirit has been seen sitting in a pew toward the middle of the church. Her presence has been felt in the form of cold drafts right in the spot where she sat. Inexplicable shadows have been seen around the altar and other areas of the church, but nothing was as bold as another incident Smitten described.

A woman had fallen asleep while lying down in a church pew, waiting for her sister to finish organ practice one night, when something prompted her to open her eyes. She wished she hadn't, for when she did, she was greeted by a hovering, jovial male face looking straight down at her. Was it a kindly former rector? Or perhaps it was a former parishioner, such as Albert Tower, who had a special attachment to the church. He had generously donated $85,000 for construction of the church and tower back in 1888. Others believe the ghost of a jolly Scotsman named Robert Craig, who died in his eighty-third year in 1859 and is now buried in the basement of the church, also makes appearances.

Ghost in the Mystery Aisle

In 2007, just days before Halloween, a security camera at the Elting Memorial Library in New Paltz captured an unidentified moving image on film. The thirty-two-second portion of the recording was later posted on YouTube and has already been viewed by nearly a third of a million people, so it's certainly no secret that the library has a ghost. Who haunts the library and why?

Around 1800 Solomon Elting (sometimes spelled Eltinge) designed and constructed the Federal-style stone building at 93 Main Street that makes up the original part of the library. It was one of the first buildings to be located in downtown New Paltz. The Hasbrouck family purchased it in the mid-1800s and remained there until 1919, when Oscar C. Hasbrouck's widow left. Oscar had died in the building in 1899 of consumption. After that, Mrs. Hasbrouck leased rooms out, and there were several more deaths and funerals of tenants held there. Charles V. Auchmoody was a boarder who died following a stroke that left him paralyzed in 1908. In October 1910, Ludlow H. Vander Burgh's funeral services were held at the house, which was then called the Solomon Elting Homestead.

In 1920, after Mrs. Hasbrouck left, local resident Philip Lefevre Elting purchased his ancestral home to give to the community for use as a library, because the first library in town had run out of space for its growing collection. At the time, Mrs. Edmund Schoonmaker was the librarian for Elting Memorial Library. She worked there for twenty-three years and died in 1938.

In 1962, a wing was added to accommodate a children's room, and in 1978, another new wing provided needed space for a new children's room and a large historical collection. In 2004, the building was listed in the National Register of Historic Places, and two years later, another construction project commenced to renovate the existing building, put on another addition, and restore the exterior.

Paranormal activity always seems to increase during periods of renovation. The library's recent renovations may explain the ghostly image captured on the library's security camera. This haunting is so spectacular, because it was either pulled off by one very clever ghost or the timing and location of the series of flukes that accompanied it were pure coincidence. The event happened close to "Dead Time," a phrase coined by the television show *Paranormal*

State and described earlier in this book (see page 11). Some para-normal experts believe that 3:00 A.M., or Dead Time, is the most active time for spirits. The library ghost appeared on film at about 3:30 A.M. The time of year is believed to be a factor as well; the incident took place a week before Halloween and the library had recently erected a temporary display for its Day of the Dead cele-bration. The image caught on film was in the oldest part of the building in the *mystery* section! It seems to pause in front of a shelf with titles, according to the *New York Times*, like *A Gathering of Ghosts* and *Still among the Living*.

The events leading to the discovery of the ghost on film occurred as follows. Jesse Chance, the circulation manager, arrived at work on the morning of October 25, 2007, to find that the front door in the old stone house portion of the library was unlatched and the alarm was turned off. Thinking there might be a security breach, he pulled up the surveillance video for that part of the library and discovered that a board member had, in fact, left through the front door the previous night after a meeting and hadn't secured it behind him. But as Chance began rewinding the tape, another moving image caught his eye. At around 3:30 A.M., a hazy, translucent, gray figure made its entrance, moving from the stairs towards the book-shelves, pausing, and then moving toward the door before disap-pearing through the east wall, all in just a half minute. Chance couldn't believe his eyes, so he saved that portion of the surveil-lance video to the computer and showed the staff. Possible expla-nations have included shadows, bugs, and dust particles. Others viewing the video closely believe the figure moves more like a human. A clerk at the library checked the lens thoroughly to rule out any imperfections and attempted to recreate the anomaly on film using various objects, but to no avail. No source for the anom-aly has been found.

Nine O'Clock Ritual

I've written stories before about police officers coming across some pretty strange sights on their rounds, like in my own hometown where officers reported that their squad cars' radio frequencies go haywire when passing a certain cemetery gate at night. The job of a policeman or security guard requires one to sometimes patrol in the middle of the night, watching for anything suspicious in vacant old houses, after-hours businesses, and cemeteries—places where vandals or mischievous kids may lurk. Coincidentally, ghosts happen to lurk in those very same places; so law enforcement officers bear witness to paranormal incidents more often than you might think. This is what happened at Fort Decker, the oldest house in the city of Port Jervis.

In 2001, according to author Linda Zimmerman, the Port Jervis police department had set up a roadblock near the Fort Decker Museum of History to prevent traffic from crossing the bridge over the railroad tracks on West Main during maintenance of the overpass. The officers on duty reportedly watched lights in the vacant Fort Decker go on and off all night, a phenomenon neighbors had been reporting for many years. Many people have seen the lights go on and off quickly in each successive room starting around 9 P.M., as if someone is walking through the house checking in on each room before retiring for the night. The house, however, is secured with an alarm system, and no one is there during the night. Zimmerman was told by museum staff that at the height of the mysterious incidents, a relative of a former occupant stopped by the museum and provided information that might shed some light on such occurrences. Apparently, the matriarch of that family followed the same routine every night, checking each room around 9 P.M. before bedtime.

Fort Decker was built at 127 West Main Street from the remains of the original structure, a military trading post and unofficial fortification that Dutch settler Frederick Haynes constructed around 1760. Haynes's wife's family, the Deckers, acquired the one-and-a-half-story stone-and-log fort when Haynes left the area in 1775. Four years later, in the midst of the Revolutionary War, the building was targeted and burned in a raid on the settlement by Joseph Brant, a Mohawk leader and military officer for the British. Brant had turned his assigned mission to search for provisions and gather intelligence on American battle plans into a justification for burning down the original fort of the Deckers on July 19, 1779. The patriots attempted to retaliate a few days later, but were badly defeated by Brant at the Battle of Minisink.

In 1793, Lt. Martinus Decker fashioned the old stone house now called Fort Decker out of stones from his family's original fort.

During construction of the Delaware and Hudson Canal in 1826, the house served as a tavern and hotel accommodating canal engineers, including one of the chief engineers, John B. Jervis, for whom the city is named. (In 1827, the community of Carpenter's Point officially changed its name to Port Jervis.) Fort Decker remained in various private hands, including the woman who obsessively made her nine o'clock rounds each night, until the Minisink Valley Historical Society purchased it in 1970 for $1,000 and converted it into their museum. The Fort Decker Museum of History is open the last Saturday of each month, May through November, and by appointment.

Aside from the frequent appearance of spook lights from within, there also have been numerous complaints over the years of the security alarm tripping, although the company that installed the units found them to be in proper working order. People have heard the sound of the ancient floorboards creaking, as if some invisible weight is bearing down on them. Doors frequently open on their own. Orbs appear in countless photographs and have been seen darting about on video. EMF readings reveal unaccountable spikes and numerous erratic energy fields.

Bigfoot of the Ice Caves

On a snowy day in the winter of 1985, two women decided to go for a leisurely drive up to the teeny hamlet of Cragsmoor on the Shawangunk Ridge. As fate would have it, they found themselves stopping at the entrance to Ice Caves Mountain longing to walk through the virgin snow. The rare ice caves of the Shawangunks are tectonic, in that they were formed as a large piece of the mountain pulled away, leaving in its wake giant fissures and cracks where snowdrifts and ice may remain throughout the year.

Although the attraction was closed for the season and nobody else was in sight, the women parked their car, stepped over the gate, and headed toward the forest, chatting casually as they walked along. Drawing closer to the woods, they noticed a large furry or hairy being that appeared "absolutely human looking" and walking upright, according to report #8064 (Class A) of the Bigfoot Field Researchers Organization (BFRO). The creature stopped in its tracks upon spotting the women, and they also stopped, as surprised to see it as it was to see them. They were only about a hundred and fifty feet away from each other. It wasn't until one of the ladies opened her mouth to ask her friend if she saw the creature that it finally broke its reciprocal stare and lumbered away at a rapid gait. It didn't run, according to the report, but it walked quickly and purposefully with a "very long stride," pausing only to turn back and look once more at the intruders to its winter sanctuary as it disappeared into the woods.

Based on the physical and behavioral description provided by the witnesses regarding the creature they saw on Ice Caves Mountain, it is believed to have been a Bigfoot. It was a hairy, massive, bipedal primate with a distinctive gait. Behavioral traits carefully documented by the BFRO, based on other sightings, further support the belief that Ice Caves Mountain harbored a bonafide Bigfoot and perhaps still does. For example, sensing no threat from the two unarmed young women, the creature paused and seemed to be sizing them up for a moment or two. BFRO says that in human encounters, Bigfoot is known to react in a more relaxed manner toward women and children, while avoiding men. Furthermore, Bigfoot is typically "unaggressive to a fault," much like the creature the women saw on Ice Caves Mountain.

A quarter of a century later, Craigsmoor, with its population of fewer than five hundred, and Ice Caves Mountain in particular, has just the right demographic and geographic features to attract a reclusive species like Bigfoot—a sparse population, mountains, woodlands, crevices in which to hide, and year-round, air-conditioned ice caves. Perhaps he will turn up again.

Unidentified Graveyard Ghosts

In 1868, a shocking train accident occurred on the Erie Rail at Carr's Rock, now known as Parker's Glen in Pike County, Pennsylvania, not far from Port Jervis in New York. A broken railroad track caused the horrific derailment known as the Erie Slaughter. Several sleeping cars plummeted down an embankment on top of each other, killing twenty-seven passengers and injuring many dozens more. Of those killed, several were interred at the nearby Laurel Grove Cemetery in Port Jervis, but others were unidentifiable because their remains were so charred. For example, on Monday, April 21, the *New York Times* reported, "Yesterday the body of . . . the unclaimed, unrecognized male remains which have lain in the dead-house since the day of the fatality were interred in the Laurel Grove Cemetery." Later, on May 4, the *Times* said, "The body hitherto supposed to be that of Raphael Strauss, of Paris, is that of Joseph E. Norwood, of Chicago, who was identified by friends who were in search of him." The article continued, "It is now supposed that the burnt body of the unknown person interred in Laurel Grove Cemetery is that of Strauss."

Many of these unidentified victims of the Erie Slaughter were also buried in Laurel Grove Cemetery, founded by Dr. John Conkling and opened on July 15, 1856. New York City landscape architects Howard Daniels and B. F. Hathaway were hired to design a lovely, garden-style cemetery where the dead could rest in peace, and the living could stroll along serene, winding, tree-lined roads and perhaps even enjoy a picnic. By 1925, some fifteen thousand people had been buried in the thirty-five-acre cemetery on East Main Street. After decades of neglect and vandalism, the grounds are currently being restored to their original splendor, and visitors can marvel at the Victorian mortuary art gracing the cemetery's tombstones, monuments, and mausoleums.

But be on the lookout for a woman in a long gown, especially if she appears to be moving too fluidly to be walking. Many people have seen an apparition of a young woman in a long, old-fashioned dress drifting through the grounds, and a couple of policemen thought she looked so real that they actually approached her to ask if she'd seen a youngster they were looking for in the cemetery, according to author Linda Zimmerman in her *Ghost Investigator, Volume 1*. The lady then floated away from them and vanished before their eyes! She is believed to be one of the victims of the Erie train tragedy, wandering around aimlessly, unaware that she's even dead.

The floating woman may also be a discontented young wife who died under other circumstances. In 1892, John F. Burgin was in the church at her funeral when a policeman showed up with a warrant for his arrest. He was allowed to view the interment at the cemetery, under the watchful eye of the constable, but then he was sent directly to jail. His father-in-law had claimed that Burgin stole $330 worth of jewelry from him. Imagine the shock to Burgin's deceased wife—first to die so young and then to witness her husband being led from her funeral to prison? And she's expected to rest in peace *how*?

Another potential candidate for the female apparition is one Madame Laura Sweitzer. Laura von Puffnitz Steinburg was born to an honorable German family in 1819. When she was just sixteen years old, she met a handsome young nobleman, Count Frederick Kolstedt Schleswick Sweitzer, who was as well-educated as she, but far poorer. To the love-struck young girl, money didn't matter, but to her father it did, and he forbade her to entertain ideas of marrying the count. He even went so far as to send her far away to a convent to ensure that the two remained separated. Somehow she found a way to get word out to her lover to let him know where she was, and he followed. He was soon hired as a gardener at the convent, which enabled him to see Laura every day, until her father became suspicious. One day, when Laura and Frederick were in the convent garden talking quietly, Laura's father appeared and a gunfight ensued. The old man was severely injured, and the couple ran off, got married, and moved to America. For a number of years, they did fine and lived comfortably. Then Frederick's health began to fail, so the couple moved to Port Jervis where Madame Sweitzer was forced to beg for money or peddle matches to the farmers. One day, "the Countess," as they called her in Port Jervis, met a horrible death that occurred so fast that she may not have realized she died. The *New York Times* of December 26, 1881, said:

> She was trying to steal a ride on the night freight train to Middletown, 35 miles south of Port Jervis, when she fell under the engine and was so crushed that her body was scarcely recognizable. Her husband died a few years [before her], and she has been buried beside him in Laurel Grove Cemetery.

There are other types of paranormal phenomena occurring at the cemetery that may be the work of either male or female spirits. People have seen strange lights, believed to be orbs. Others have been touched lightly, as if being tickled by a feather, but no source can be found for the sensation. EMF readings have been taken by multiple paranormal investigators; one such investigator was thrilled to actually see her first full-bodied apparition after years of investigating. Batteries of flashlights and cameras have reportedly died, and equipment often malfunctions. Numerous photographs and video footage reveal anomalies believed to be paranormal in nature.

At the Laurel Grove Cemetery, hauntings have been reported for nearly as long as the cemetery has been in existence. For those who seek out ghosts or document the alleged reports of their appearances, places like Laurel Grove Cemetery are very appealing to research and investigate. But not everyone shares this enthusiasm. I leave you with this final incident, from the *New York Times* of April 9, 1898, regarding Laurel Grove's effect on a man who was perhaps haunted by one ghost too many: "John Burkhart of Port Jervis, keeper of the Laurel Grove Cemetery, built a gallows in his house and then called in police officers to see how he intended to end his life in a fortnight. His wife caused his arrest, and he will be brought to the State Hospital here."

A President Phantom in the Orchard

If one were lucky enough to visit Lindenwald, the thirty-six-room mansion built in 1797 by Judge William Peter Van Ness, he or she might meet the ghost of a former chief executive. Martin Van Buren, the nation's eighth president, was born in nearby Kinderhook in 1782. He moved into this Federal-style mansion in 1839 during his first and only term of office; he ran and lost two more presidential campaigns before retiring from public service. During his retirement, he discovered the joys of farming on his 125-acre estate, with its bountiful apple orchards; he famously insisted that he preferred to be remembered as just a farmer rather than an ex-president.

Van Buren's four sons—Abraham, Martin Jr., Smith, and John—shared the mansion at Lindenwald with him. Son John was a compulsive gambler who waged and lost his lady friend, Madame Ameriga Vespucci, in a game of cards against George Parish at another haunted location, the John Hoover Inn in Evans Mills, New York.

President Van Buren died at Lindenwald in his seventy-ninth year on July 24, 1862. The *New York Times* that week described the funeral arrangements as such:

> The pleasant little village of Kinderhook, on the far up Hudson, long since made famous as the birthplace and residence of Martin Van Buren, the boon-companion, friend, counselor, and successor in office of Andrew Jackson, yesterday paid her last earthly honors to her favorite son. While in other portions of the country, the thousands of flags waving at half-mast bespoke the sorrow of a nation at the loss of an ex-President, in the village of Kinderhook the emblems of mourning were of a more heartfelt character, and betokened a deeper sorrow at the loss of an old neighbor, a kind friend, and an esteemed citizen. . . . At 12 o'clock preliminary services were held at Lindenwald, the mansion of the deceased, a mile and a half south of the village. . . . After the services, the family and near relatives and friends of the deceased took a last look at the remains previous to their being conveyed to the church.

Shortly after Van Buren's passing, John wagered Lindenwald in a game of cards and lost it to a New York City financier named L. Jerome. Jerome's family, including daughter Jenny Jerome—who would later give birth to Winston Churchill—then moved to the estate. Meanwhile, John had traveled to Europe but died on the return voyage from England to New York City.

In 1873, just eleven years after President Van Buren's passing, Lindenwald was sold by George Wilder to James Van Alstyne and John Van Buren (a namesake of the president's son) for just $32,000—an outrageously small price to pay, even then, for a house, furniture, horses, carriages, farm, and a couple hundred acres. That's apparently enough to make a president rise from his grave.

Van Buren's spirit has been seen roaming around the property, especially in the old apple orchards that once dotted the landscape. But his is not the only spirit believed to haunt the estate. He is joined by buddy Aaron Burr, whose spirit was also seen walking among the apple trees in the orchard. Van Buren's butler, who hanged himself in the orchard, also haunts the grounds; his ethereal likeness was seen hanging from one particular tree.

Inside, previous owners reportedly heard mysterious footsteps and heavy, solid wood doors opening and closing effortlessly with nobody near them. Unexplained odors, like buttery pancakes and perfume, for which no source can be found, appear out of nowhere.

Violin music and female voices have been heard and luminous feminine figures have been seen at the feet of various occupants' beds.

Nevertheless, Lindenwald, now the Martin Van Buren National Historic Site, is a must-see for history buffs and paranormal enthusiasts alike. It is listed in the National Register of Historic Places and governed by the National Park Service, which operates a visitor center in the mansion and provides ranger-guided tours of the property.

Scared to Death

On June 10, 1894, the *New York Times* ran the following description of Kingston's Old Dutch Church:

> More than two centuries ago, when the site of the beautiful City of Kingston was in the midst of an almost trackless wilderness, a little colony of God-fearing Hollanders settled on the spot and in a short time founded a church. Around this sacred edifice a cemetery gradually sprang up. The primitive church has long since passed away, and in its place one of the finest church buildings in the city lifts its spire toward the clouds; but the graves have been undisturbed.

Au contraire. The graves *were*, in fact, disturbed when the Dutch congregation that has held the property on the corner of Wall and Main streets in Kingston since 1659 built their fourth church there in 1852. According to the current pastor, Ken Walsh, it was necessary to dig foundation ditches through the cemetery to build the church, which meant leaving dozens of unmarked, forgotten graves under the foundation of the church. The most famous burial there was New York State's first governor, George Clinton. But the earliest burial record dates to 1710, so the first interment is believed to have been around the same time that the original church was built on the property. A June 10, 1894, *New York Times* article said that excavations made years prior indicated that many people had been buried very early in the church's history, because skeletons piled "three and four deep" nearly crumbled into dust when lifted. The fragile remains were reburied in the cemetery in countless unnamed graves. The *Times* article also stated that in 1885, when an addition was being added to the chapel, "many fragments of coffins containing a few blackened bones were exposed." So the graves in Old Dutch Cemetery and beneath the sanctuary most certainly have been disturbed, not once but several times in the course of the church's lengthy history. When the rapidly occurring deaths from Kingston's cholera epidemic caused the cemetery to reach its capacity in the mid-1800s, burials ceased.

Pastor Walsh told the *Times Herald-Record* that he has seen strange, shadowy figures in the stairway and has felt a subtle stroking of his face in the study. But subtle touches and vague shadows are nothing compared to the creepy legend most often associated with the historic church. It all began with the "hobgoblin in the steeple," says the church's own Web site. According to legend, an early pastor of the church was returning by boat on the Hudson River to Kingston with his wife when a hideous hobgoblin suddenly appeared, perching threateningly on the vessel's bowsprit, apparently leering at passengers and crew. To quiet his hysterical wife, the pastor performed a hasty exorcism, which seemed to do the trick. The creature, whatever it was, disappeared. The next morning, the goblin's hat was found hanging off the steeple of the Old Dutch Church. Some took this as a sign that the goblin was trapped in the steeple and has been deprived of its evil powers ever since. Every Sunday morning for many years, strange, throaty sounds would interrupt the sermon.

In the 1850s, a man painting the steeple suddenly became violently ill and died. Some said he died from painter's colic (lead poisoning), but others insisted that the hobgoblin revealed its horrible face through the window of the steeple, literally scaring the painter to death. Now the painter has joined the hobgoblin in haunting the church. Upstanding nineteenth-century citizens swore that they saw a spectral painter working on the steeple in the midst of lightning flashes. In 1984, when the steeple needed a fresh coat of paint, the unfortunate painter chosen to do the task didn't last long before he clambered down the scaffolding, saying that something had tapped him three times on the shoulder. Had he turned around instead of scurrying down as he did, would he have seen the spirit of the last man who attempted to paint the steeple? Or would he have seen the hobgoblin, hoping to scare another victim to death?

UFO Capital of the Northeast

For a tiny hamlet with a little more than six hundred houses, Pine Bush has certainly made a big name for itself in paranormal circles. The community, located in the town of Crawford in Orange County, was put on the map between the late 1970s and the early 1990s when it experienced such a flap of UFO sightings that the area was dubbed the "UFO Capital of the Northeast" and one of the world's "UFO hotspots." In fact, the famous author and abductee Whitley Streiber was taken from his cabin near Pine Bush and subsequently wrote *Communion: A True Story*. Not only were there near-nightly reports of UFO sightings—especially so-called "triangles" and boomerang-shaped spacecraft—but there was also an increase in alleged close encounters with extraterrestrials, alien abductions, Bigfoot sightings, hauntings, and sightings of otherworldly beings.

While the entire Hudson Valley region has been a UFO magnet since at least the 1950s, Pine Bush experienced its most activity in the 1980s, beginning with a spectacular light show in the skies over the town of Kent on December 31, 1982, which occurred just moments before the customary dropping of the ball in Times Square one hour south of there. Hence, the New Year arrived simultaneously with the official commencement of the famous Hudson Valley UFO flap. That phenomenon yielded upwards of seven thousand sightings of primarily boomerang-shaped spaceships in the skies of New York and Connecticut over the course of thirteen years.

Not long after the Kent incident, a retired policeman reported an odd grouping of multicolored lights moving lazily over the Hudson Valley area, humming almost inaudibly. The object moved so slowly over his house that he was able to determine, without a doubt, that the V-shaped arrangement of lights was on the same massive spacecraft. Reports of UFO sightings then snowballed to the tune of hundreds over the next few years. March 24, 1983, was a record day for phone calls to a UFO hotline in the area. More than three hundred people called in saying they had seen something unbelievable and unexplainable in the skies that night—a humongous "flying city," as one observer put it. Another witness said it was the size of three football fields combined. All agreed that what they saw was silent and slow-moving. The *Westchester-Rockland Daily Item* ran the headline, "Hundreds Claim to Have Seen UFO."

There was a period in the mid-1980s when hundreds of UFO enthusiasts converged on the West Searsville Road nightly in hopes of seeing a UFO. They were rarely disappointed. Soon traffic became hazardous, prompting local law enforcement to ban any further parking along that stretch. Generally, the UFOs reported that year in the Crawford and Pine Bush area were slow, large, and very quiet. Often they departed at alarming speeds not yet possible with the technology of modern man. An episode of the television show *Unsolved Mysteries* told of an enormous boomerang-shaped spacecraft that hovered over the Newburgh mall in broad daylight. J. Allen Hynek, Philip J. Imbrogno, and Bob Pratt penned a book in response to the public interest of that UFO uproar called *Night Siege: The Hudson Valley UFO Sightings*.

Although it's somewhat quieter in the skies over Pine Bush these days, the name of the little hamlet will forever be synonymous with UFO sightings, which bodes well for at least three local businesses—the Burlingham Inn, a "UFO bed and breakfast"; the Cup and Saucer Diner, and Butch's UFO Barbershop. Enthusiasts still watch the skies, knowing that it's no longer a matter of *if* they will see a UFO, but when.

Beware of Bannerman's Island

There are many ancient accounts of Native Americans believing Bannerman's Island was haunted by powerful spirits of the dead that created the sometimes unforgiving conditions of the water surrounding the island. There were deadly undercurrents, fierce winds that seemed to come out of nowhere, and dangerous choppy waters. The Indians came to believe that the conditions were manipulated by those spirits, under the guise of natural elements, to keep intruders away. Though such stories are steeped in legend, it's a fact that Indians at least attempted to live on the island before the early Dutch explorers arrived. Archaeological digs have yielded evidence of Indian encampments with few artifacts left behind, which indicates a possible hasty departure. Had the powerful evil spirits they believed inhabited the island frightened them off? Or had they been scared away by the fiendish Heer of the Dunderberg? In "The Storm-Ship," Washington Irving painted the Heer of the Donder Berg as the mother of all goblins, a malevolent, possessive entity capable of conjuring the deadly storms around its precious island and the Hudson Highlands.

The early Dutch believed Bannerman's Island, halfway between Beacon and Cold Spring, marked the northern gate of the Heer's domain. They went to great lengths when passing the island to shield themselves from the goblin king by hiding or ducking out of sight. Once they were safely past the island, they could breathe a sigh of relief. Intoxicated sailors were purportedly dropped off on the island to sober up and later retrieved. What horrors they witnessed in their drunken state will never be known, for the alcohol numbed their senses and distorted their memories of the allegedly inhospitable island. During the Revolutionary War, sixty-foot logs, pointed at the tip, were stood on end with the pointy side up and submerged just below the surface of the water at Bannerman's Island to gouge the hulls of British ships attempting to enter the Hudson Highlands, an action that held more true risk than a chance encounter with the Heer of the Dunderberg.

So the island had acquired a sinister reputation by the Dutch and Native Americans before Scotsman Francis Bannerman decided to buy it in 1900. The wealthy arms dealer paid no mind to stories of ghosts, goblins, or other supernatural beings. There were castles to build and explosives to move. His enormous New York City warehouse and munitions museum had run out of space for an ever-increasing stock after he purchased ninety percent of the surplus equipment and ammunition from the Spanish-American War. The middle of nation's largest city was not the ideal place to store explosives anyway. Bannerman relocated his surplus equipment and ammunition to the six-and-a-half-acre island's new storage buildings, including the most visible, Bannerman Castle. He also had a residential castle built, along with a lodge, employee quarters, workshops, and other buildings.

To create the island's docks, Bannerman acquired old ships that he sank along the shore before covering them in concrete. One tugboat captain agreed to sell his boat to Bannerman, as long as the workers waited until he was well out of sight before sinking it— a fair request, because the captain couldn't bear to see his own vessel go down. The thoughtless workers didn't honor the request. The good captain had barely begun to walk away when his tugboat began sinking. He turned and cursed Bannerman and the insensitive crew, telling them they hadn't heard the last of him. Sometime later there were reports that the workers could hear the distinct double-ringing of a ship's bell, meaning it was going in reverse, while standing in the lodge built over the sunken boat. With the late captain's threat still on their minds, they wondered if perhaps he had returned from the dead and was attempting to bring his beloved tugboat back up to the surface.

Bannerman himself was far more considerate than his crew. In his obituary in the *New York Times* on November 28, 1918, it was reported that he donated $100,000 worth of military supplies to the king of England for the Scotch National Guardsmen following an attack by German forces in 1914. He then donated two cannons and $20,000 more to the United States government two months before his death. In fact, his acts of goodwill that year are believed to have caused his demise. The *Times* said, "A few weeks ago, Mr. Bannerman donated 50,000 garments to the Belgium Relief Commission . . . it was said that the strain of overwork to which he was subjected in connection with the procurement and shipment of this gift was immediately responsible for his death." While construction ceased when the patriarch died, his family continued spending lazy summers on their island retreat, enjoying its gardens and the serenity. But on one sultry summer day, August 15, 1920, a mysterious explosion of two hundred pounds of gunpowder and shells in the powder house reverberated up and down the Hudson River and forever altered the landscape of Bannerman's Island. Mrs. Bannerman, her sister, and the island superintendent were all injured, but incredibly no one died. The damage to the structures Bannerman had carefully planned and laid out, however, was immense. The *New York Times* of August 16, 1920, described the destruction:

> The island . . . was "fortified" by a high stone wall, of which a section twenty-five feet long was blown to the mainland, blocking the New York Central Railroad tracks which run along the Hudson River bank nearby. The Bannerman "Castle," which occupies the central portion of the island was considerably damaged, window panes being smashed, shutters blown from their hangings and part of the tower blown far out into the river. . . . A corner of the Bannerman Island near the powder house was blown into the river. The cause of the explosion had not been learned tonight, but residents of the neighborhood attributed it to river pirates.

The Bannerman family sporadically visited the island, such as it was, until the 1930s, when they vacated for good. New York State purchased it in 1967, and two years later, another mysterious incident caused even further damage to the crumbling structures. A fire of unknown origin burned what was left of the buildings, and the island, deemed unsafe like centuries before, was declared off-limits to the public. Was it the work of an eternally disgruntled tugboat captain with a bone to pick or the nasty Heer of the Dunderberg reclaiming his territory? Or does something else haunt Bannerman's Island? Photographs of its abandoned buildings and grounds reveal hundreds of orbs and even spirit faces. Perhaps drunken sailors really were left on the island as a "peace offering" to the almighty Heer, to keep him, shall we say, occupied, while the rest of the crew continued to safely pass the island. Or maybe more people died in the choppy waters surrounding the island prior to the printing press than we'll ever know.

I also came across an interesting online article from *Mysteries of the Hudson Valley, 1995–1996* called "Near Bannerman's Island: Tale of a Shelled Killer." Apparently in 1988 and 1989, residents of Cold Spring and Garrison began reporting their pets missing, both dogs and cats. When jumbled piles of skeletal remains were found increasingly along the shores of the Hudson River, citizens grew understandably concerned that something either supernatural or satanic was happening. In either case, it didn't take long to suspect Bannerman's Island, thanks to its long history of eerie lore. At one point, a rumor began circulating about a strange creature coming up on shore and mutilating stray animals. When people heard dogs howling as if in agony for three nights in a row, they dubbed the alleged creature the "Bannerman's Island Monster." Luckily, the monster seems to have gone back into hiding, as things have since quieted down considerably.

Today, Bannerman's Island is owned by the New York State Office of Parks, Recreation, and Historic Preservation and is mostly in ruins. Though many of the exterior walls remain, they are but a shell of the original structures, with the interiors long since burned down. The island has been deemed unsafe, because of vandalism and neglect. The submerged causeways and old ships have produced dangerous obstacles to navigate around, so the castle may only be visited during guided tours offered by the Bannerman's

Castle Trust, the current caretakers. If you happen to take a south-bound train through the area, you can see the old Bannerman's Castle with its huge sign still clearly visible after all these years.

Crueler Than Death

There once stood an old stone house in the tiny hamlet of Leeds near the town of Catskill, where a man lived for nearly three-quarters of a century with a noose tied around his neck to remind both himself and his neighbors of a crime he allegedly committed in the early 1700s. This crime, some say, left his property haunted by an unearthly, laughing spirit.

Ralph Sutherland was a hard man to work for—violent, miserable, and unyielding—so it was inevitable that his young servant girl would eventually muster the courage to attempt an escape. No one could possibly go on living with the way he had treated her. Sutherland was unable to acquire an American servant, so he paid the passage fee for a Scotchwoman who agreed to serve him at least until the fee was repaid. Had she known about his raging temper, and the fact that he would hold her virtually in bondage, she never would have accepted the offer.

One day when Sutherland was preoccupied, the girl took off on foot, sprinting toward freedom. You can imagine his fury when Sutherland discovered his servant missing. How dare she, after all he had done for her! He mounted his horse and set off in search of the girl, but the longer he rode, the angrier he became. By the time he caught up to the terrified girl, he was blind with rage. He later admitted that he tied the girl's wrists to the horse's tail and set off toward his house at a slow gallop, never intending to kill her, but only to drag her a short distance as punishment. At some point, his plan went awry, and the horse began racing at an inhuman speed. Few alternative scenarios could explain how her lifeless body had become so terribly mangled. Sutherland swore that it was an accident, saying the girl had stumbled against the horse's hind legs, spooking it, which caused it to charge. He'd been thrown from the saddle, he insisted, while the girl was dragged off violently through the brush, repeatedly crashing against the rocks and trees of the rugged landscape. His audacity to blame the victim for the shocking stunt, when he was the one cruel enough in the first place to tie her to the horse, only made his neighbors more certain of his guilt.

Sutherland was sentenced to be hanged, but a few influential relatives were able to convince the court that they couldn't condemn a man to die based purely on circumstantial evidence. He was the only living witness. So it was decided, by some curious stroke of inspiration, that sentencing would be delayed until Sutherland's ninety-ninth birthday. The convicted man, however, was ordered to wear a hangman's noose around his neck continuously without exception until that time. The *Auburn Citizen* called it "A Strange Sentence" in their article of January 7, 1908, saying the punishment "was a more cruel decision than the sentence of immediate death would have been, but it was no doubt in harmony with the spirit of the times." Sutherland was further ordered to appear before the Catskill judges once a year to prove he was following the court's order, which he did dependably. But it wasn't necessary. Everyone in town knew he obeyed his presentencing orders, for they saw him in public with the silken cord always knotted around his throat. No one had ever seen him without it.

The man became reclusive, for the most part, and rarely spoke a word to anyone with whom he came in contact. Passersby avoided his house at night, because there were rumors that it had become haunted by the servant girl. Charles M. Skinner, in his *Legends of Our Own Land* series of 1896, wrote:

> After dark his house was avoided, for gossips said that a shrieking woman passed it nightly, tied at the tail of a giant horse with fiery eyes and smoking nostrils; that a skeleton in a winding sheet had been found there; that a curious thing, somewhat like a woman, had been known to sit on his garden wall with lights shining from her fingertips, uttering unearthly laughter; and that domestic animals reproached the man by groaning and howling beneath his windows.

Sutherland went on to live far longer than any court ever expected him to, so when his ninety-ninth birthday arrived, there was nobody willing to abide by the bizarre plan to sentence a ninety-nine-year-old man. He had outlived all of his accusers, and he had certainly been haunted by his crime all those years, which was punishment enough. Still, he refused to remove the now-familiar noose. The *Auburn Citizen* said, "the spirit of self punishment continued, and when Sutherland, after he had passed his hundredth year, was discovered dead alone in his house, his throat was found to be encircled by the rope which had been placed there nearly three-quarters of a century before."

The Shanley Hotel

The Shanley Hotel in Napanoch has thirty-five rooms and a basement with hidden passageways, but this wasn't the first building on the spot. The first hotel at 56 Main Street was the work of Thomas Rich, who endeavored in 1845 to build the grandest hotel in the Hudson Valley. His efforts paid off handsomely. The inn on the corner attracted train passengers, city folk from nearby New York City, and the regulars in town. Then fifty years later, a fire nearby spread to the hotel and burned it to the ground. There were no casualties from the fire, but there have been numerous deaths, both documented and rumored, that have since occurred.

The three-story Napanoch Hotel was promptly built on the original hotel's foundation. In 1906, Irishman James Louis Shanley, who hailed from a family of successful restaurateurs and hoteliers, and his wife Beatrice purchased the hotel. Under their care, it became the envy of the region, frequented by such patrons as Eleanor Roosevelt and Thomas Edison. In an effort to provide everything a respectable customer might desire, the Shanleys added a barbershop, billiard room, and bowling alley to the hotel. For those seeking desires of a different nature, the hotel sidelined as a popular speakeasy and bordello. The current owners, the Nicosias, have authentically restored the bordello for your enjoyment. Not that kind of enjoyment! I'm talking about paranormal enjoyment, as the bordello is said to be the most haunted room at the inn! You've heard the phrase, "if these walls could talk." Well, rest assured, the walls of the bordello, and every room in the Shanley Hotel, talk.

As good as things were for the Shanleys, they had their share of heartbreak, as did their patrons and employees. They lost three children before they reached the age of nine months. For instance, baby Kathleen died after two weeks of severe spinal meningitis. Beatrice's sister, Esther Faughnan, who lived in an apartment in the hotel, died there giving birth to her third child. The Shanleys then raised Esther's two surviving little girls, ages five and six, as their own. The hotel's barber also suffered the loss of a child. It was reported in the *Middletown Daily Times* on May 31, 1911:

> A four year old daughter of Peter Gregory, who is a barber at the Shanley Hotel, Napanoch, fell into a well on the farm of Louis A. Hoornbeck on Saturday and was drowned. The child had lifted up the lid and fell head first into the spring. The body was found two hours afterward.

During a recent paranormal investigation at the Shanley, a psychic in the group mentioned aloud that she was sensing babies or childbirth, and she asked if the room had something to do with either. Just as she formed the question, every single K2 meter in the room shot straight off the chart, indicating a large amount of electromagnetic energy. The psychic's words seemingly hit a nerve with a spirit presence in the room. Because of the evidence collected, the group involved believes it is the room that either Mrs. Shanley's babies were in when they died, or (perhaps more likely) that it was Esther's room, where she died during childbirth.

In 1937, James Shanley died of a massive coronary at sixty-two, and the funeral was held in the hotel. Four years later, the widowed Beatrice decided her heart was no longer in the hotel business, not without her partner. In 1944, the Hazens became the new proprietors, and Beatrice moved to New York City. Today, the Nicosias are doing a fantastic job renovating the hotel to the splendor of its heyday. They quickly learned that it was incredibly haunted by many spirits with different stories, so they found their niche by promoting ghost investigations and events to allow people to acquire their own evidence and judge for themselves.

Footsteps are often heard going up and down stairways and hallways, doors (and there are a lot of them) open and close when nobody is anywhere near them, and people report being poked or stroked on the cheek, especially in "Joe's Room." Joe is a character who used to live at the Shanley, and all that remains in his third-floor room today is his chair. They say that he doesn't like anyone to sit in his chair without asking him, and when women sit there, they sometimes feel a gentle nudge against their shoulder or a ticklish stroke against their cheek. EVPs have been captured in the

"Gentlemen's Quarters." Apparitions have been seen and captured on film. Rocking chairs, balls, and toys move when nobody can be seen around them. Temperature variations often accompany the feeling of being watched. People visiting the room known as the bordello experience light-headedness, shortness of breath, and intensified feelings. Much of the evidence captured by the Nicosias and visitors is posted on their Web site for all to enjoy. Visit www.shanleyhotel.com, if you dare.

That's No Ape!

It's a squirrel! It's a chimp! No, it's Baby Bigfoot! A video was taken at an outdoor rock concert in November 2005 at Lembo Lake in Modena that inadvertently captured what appears to be a mother and child of the Bigfoot variety, silhouetted in trees on the horizon. That famous video has been called the "New York Baby Footage," or the "Doug Pridgen Footage," for the camper who videotaped it.

Several years after the Wamboozy Rock and Roll Consciousness Festival that yielded the incredible footage, Pridgen wanted to transfer his grainy 8mm tape to VHS, so he hooked his camcorder up to his big-screen television before going into the other room. Meanwhile, his girlfriend walked into the room. When the footage got to the part showing Pridgen's drinking buddy talking with animated gestures beside a campfire, his girlfriend noticed something moving in the tree line about a hundred feet behind the oblivious campers. On closer inspection, it was obviously something swinging in the tree, from branch to branch, and climbing up and down effortlessly. She called Pridgen into the room and asked him what it was, and then they noticed another figure in the tree, as well. It was larger and less active than the little guy. It was the first time Pridgen had seen the footage, since he hadn't noticed it while he was filming his friend.

The famous footage was shot in an apple grove at Lembo Lake campground, owned by Michael Lembo Sr. One hundred to two hundred people were on the property for the music festival, but Lembo's rules were strict for campers. As each vehicle arrived, it was searched at the entrance to make sure no glass containers or animals (including apes and such) were being brought on the property, for obvious safety reasons. So, Lembo and Pridgen were as baffled as the next guy about what they saw on the film. Were they some type of apes, they wondered? That would be unusual for New York State. Were they humans imitating monkeys? Humans can't swing like that! Analysis of the video by some experts in both zoology and photography found it to be authentic, ruling out the human theory. So what were they? Obviously, Bigfoot came to many people's minds, especially because the Hudson Valley has a history of harboring such cryptids.

By returning to the scene and measuring the height of the trees and the statistics with a careful frame-by-frame inspection of the video footage, researchers determined an approximate size of the smaller being: Baby Bigfoot was about three or four feet tall. It first appeared coming from the back of the larger one. Then, as it zips up the tree and frolics some twenty feet off the ground, the larger one waits off to the side patiently before disappearing into the woods, no doubt keeping a cautious eye on the little guy. Was it a mother Bigfoot and her youngling? Some believe so.

According to the Bigfoot Field Researchers Organization, which assigned Report #7514 (Class B) to Pridgen's Bigfoot case, the young of the species are "allowed to explore and be potentially visible" in cases where the adult can remain undetectable. They must be intelligent enough to know that their youth are harder to identify than the distinctively huge and hairy adults.

Like Ice Caves Mountain in nearby Cragsmoor, the hamlet of Modena where Lembo Lake is located is primarily a rural community where development has been minimal, perfect for a population-shunning species like Bigfoot. Lembo Lake, off Route 44/55, is a private, three-hundred-acre former orchard that now offers fishing, camping, and ATV racing with permission.

West Point

THE UNITED STATES MILITARY ACADEMY AT WEST POINT (USMA) keeps an official "Ghost File," and for good reason. The paranormal activity reportedly experienced by several cadets in Room 4714 in 1972 prompted the Army to close the room, deeming it "off limits" even to this day. The story was so sensational that it was reported on NBC and CBS and in the *New York Times, Time, Newsweek, Life,* and countless national and local newspapers. But reports of ghosts are nothing new at West Point, the oldest of the nation's five service academies.

In 1908, when "Old Blood and Guts" himself, Gen. George S. Patton, was a cadet adjutant at the military academy, he wrote a letter to his girlfriend regarding a phantom with a mummy-like appearance that he had seen at the foot of his bed. Pershing Barracks, Nininger Hall, and the Thayer House are said to be haunted, as are several other less-publicized buildings.

Crusher in Room 4714

Cadet Cpl. Theodore Hoham, United States Cadet Corps class of 2011, has done extensive research on the ghost stories associated with West Point and has been interviewed by the *Times Herald-Record*. While he does not speak officially for the military academy (or the U.S. Army or the Department of Defense), he was kind enough to provide an abundance of information for the following stories, beginning with the famed Room 4714.

Of all the ghost stories told about West Point, the most publicized is about Room 4714 of the Scott Barracks. Named after Gen. Winfield Scott, the barracks is five stories tall, with seven floors in the northeast tower. It was built in 1938 on the former site of the nineteenth-century officers' quarters and was first called the New North Barracks and then the Old North Barracks.

The first inkling of what was to become a sensational ghost story occurred on October 20, 1972. It was reported in the December 1972 edition of the *Pointer* newsletter, written by the members of Company G-3. Cadet Jim O'Connor had gone to the latrine down the hall from Room 4714 to shower. He had just turned on the water when he noticed that his bathrobe, which was hanging on a hook, was swinging freakishly from side to side, sometimes even pausing on one side as if someone was toying with it. Simultaneously, the water in the shower had turned cold. As O'Connor stood there trying to figure it out, the robe suddenly stopped swinging, without even slowing down first. The water temperature then returned to normal. O'Connor was ready to attribute the strange incident to a draft or a fluke, until he saw the robe begin swinging vigorously again and the water again changed, this time to very hot. Needless to say, he didn't bother finishing his shower, but returned to the room he shared with Cadet Artie Victor.

The next night, Victor went to the same latrine, and when he was about to flush the urinal, he saw the handle go down without even touching it. Then the toilet paper started unrolling. Victor raced back to get his roommate. By the time the two had returned to the latrine, half of the toilet paper was strewn about the floor.

The following night O'Connor was leaving the latrine when he glanced back and saw a figure in a tattered, gray coat sitting on the toilet, holding a nineteenth-century musket. The apparition's white eyes glowed in the dim light. It then stood up and dissipated, as the terrified cadet watched.

On the evening of October 23, 1972, the two plebes had just climbed into bed in Room 4714 when the room's temperature dropped precipitously. Looking toward the window for a possible explanation, like a draft coming through a cracked window, they instead noticed a man's torso floating near the radiator in front of the window. After two minutes, it faded.

Exactly a week later, the spectral roommate returned. The sudden chill in the air was promptly followed by the same apparition coming out of the wall above one bed. It wandered around in circles for a few moments and then disappeared as it approached the two cadets.

The following night happened to be Halloween, and O'Connor and Victor were joined by their company commander and platoon leader. Just as the platoon leader lay down to sleep, the room became noticeably colder, and a shadowy profile of a head and neck appeared near the ceiling directly over him for a full two minutes. The company commander didn't see the apparition, but he felt the drop in room temperature.

On November 1, the following night, the deputy brigade adjutant volunteered to sleep there, under pressure from the lieutenant commander of Company G-4 to get to the bottom of what he called "the ghost thing." The poor guy awoke at 2:30 A.M. to a freezing room and a heavy weight on his chest. He looked up and saw an apparition of an eyeless older man wearing a long coat and a tall hat. O'Connor heard his comrade yell and came around the partition just in time to see the apparition standing on the bed and then scurry back through the wall. Feeling the spot, the men found it to be cold to the touch.

The next night, five upperclassmen invaded the room, prepared to stay awake in shifts. It wasn't long before one cadet who was lying on the floor felt a sudden pressure on his chest, rendering him unable to sit up or even lift his head to scream. On November 3, three cadets from battalion staff stayed in the room with O'Connor, and they came armed with thermocouples. The temperature readings in the room that night were all over the place, from minus-eighteen degrees Celsius to normal room temperature. On November 17, 1972, less than a month after the paranormal activity began, the *Pasco East* newspaper ran a story titled, "Army Puts West Point Ghost Room Off-Limits." The room remains closed to this day.

An official investigation in 1972 that included interviews with witnesses and the opinions of paranormal experts Lorraine and Ed Warren prompted the tactical department to close the room off as sleeping quarters. A midshipman from the rival U.S. Naval Academy attempted to claim responsibility for the antics, but his story was easily discounted. Current cadets in other rooms and buildings still experience the wrath of "Crusher," as the entity is now known. When they feel an invisible weight pressing firmly on their chests while in bed, they blame it on the ghost of Room 4714, who now apparently gets around well.

Who is Crusher? Former cadet O'Connor offered a 1993 USMA graduate three theories in an email exchange in 2004. He said there was a Colonel O'Connor, no relation to him, who burned to death in a fire near that site in the 1820s. He believed that the ghost they saw was wearing an 1823 cavalry uniform. He also mentioned that the late Jean Dixon, the famous psychic, sensed he was a Confederate spy who was hanged at Hangman's Hollow at West Point. The deputy honor committee chairman who escorted Dixon to 4714 said she was literally thrown from the room by some unseen force. Finally, the third theory was suggested by a Mormon cadet and supported by another cadet, who claimed the entity was a warlock. They found literary references in the academy's library to support the theory that the spirit was a "lieutenant of Satan, a demon of nightmares."

The General and the Mummy

Behind Pershing Barracks and just outside the cadet central area is the much smaller Nininger Hall, the last remaining structure from the old Central Barracks. Built in 1882, Nininger was then known as "1st Division," and it traditionally housed the highest-ranking cadet. When "Old Blood and Guts" himself, Gen. George S. Patton, was a cadet adjutant at West Point in 1908, he called these barracks home. While reading through Patton's archived letters to his girlfriend, which were written in that period, Cadet Cpl. Theodore Hoham recently stumbled upon a reference to a paranormal experience Patton endured. "In the letter, he relates a story in which he describes seeing a phantom with a mummy-like appearance at the foot of the bed, which beckoned to him and then disappeared," Hoham said. "Patton believed that the ghost was an ancient warrior and that the sighting of the ghost meant that he was destined for greatness in the Army." History proved the good general correct on at least the second point. Whether or not the mummy figure was an ancient warrior is anyone's guess. Some think it was the ghost of a former West Point cadet wrapped in sterile medical gauze for injuries he sustained during battle.

Patton wasn't the only general with ties to West Point who spoke of ghosts. In Gen. Douglas MacArthur's final West Point roll call and address to the Corps of Cadets in 1962, as he accepted the prestigious Sylvanus Thayer Award, he assured the audience that should the "Long Gray Line" ever fail, "a million ghosts in olive drab, in brown khaki, in blue and gray, would rise from their white crosses thundering those magic words: Duty. Honor. Country." In bidding his alma mater farewell, he predicted that when his moment came to "cross the river" to the other side, his last conscious thoughts would undoubtedly be of West Point. Perhaps the military academy is haunted because so many alumni and staff have thought about it as they took their final breath.

Stranger in the Window

The whole inner history of these transactions may never be made known. Their details are whispered between cadets at odd moments and in the dark. But a massive ignorance is displayed by the young men when questioned in regard to any of the unusual happenings.

"Spooks Invade West Point"
New York Times
August 29, 1894

A number of cadets not only believe that West Point is haunted, but have reported their own first-hand accounts. The following incident made a believer out of a cadet named Bruce.

The West Academic Building, now known as Pershing Barracks, is located immediately west of Thayer Road just north of the corner of Brewerton. Construction of the Gothic-style building (which originally had some classrooms and laboratories before becoming barracks) was hindered by a series of unfortunate incidents. The superintendent of works was fired, the contractor quit, and the architect was beset by design changes and errors in estimates. Nevertheless, the building, the largest of the nineteenth-century structures at West Point, was finished in four years and was occupied by 1895.

Bruce was on his way back to his room in Pershing Barracks one day after class when he looked up to his third-floor window and saw his roommate Eric standing there wearing his regular academic uniform. Next to him was a stranger wearing a cadet's full-dress uniform like that worn at formal affairs and in parades at West Point. The apparition was so clear that Bruce could later recall the brass breastplate and crossbelts. When he finally reached his room, he found Eric alone at his desk; the decked-out cadet was nowhere to be seen. Bruce wondered aloud how the stranger managed to leave the room without being seen, and Eric replied that he had not invited anyone in and hadn't knowingly stood at their window beside a ghost—or anyone else for that matter.

Bruce was not the first to experience something paranormal at Pershing. Many others have heard talking and strange noises emanating from the basement and say that they feel a persistent, unnatural chill there throughout the year.

Molly's Mark

During the psychic investigation of Room 4714 in 1972, the nearby Quarters 100, also called the Superintendent's House and the Thayer Home, was found to have several of its own spirits. One named Molly was the Irish maid of Col. Sylvanus Thayer, the "Father of West Point," who was superintendent of the military academy from 1817 to 1833. Thayer was the first to live in the brick Federal-style mansion. Built in 1820 for superintendents and their families, it is one of the oldest buildings still standing on base.

Molly left her mark, so to speak, on the cutting board in the first-floor kitchen, presumably in an effort to let the living know she was still among them. A persistent moist spot, wiped off each morning, would be wet again by evening one hundred and fifty years after Molly's passing. She is also presumed to be the "lady in white" who awakens the superintendent's family members and turns down the sheets for them.

According to interoffice correspondence between Superintendent William Knowlton and the USMA librarian in October 1972, one young man awoke to find a lady in a long white dress who proceeded to walk through the door when he demanded to know who she was. Molly has been blamed for nearly every unexplainable incident at the house: door-knocking, doors slamming, and small objects moving from one place to another in the middle of the night. Usually those objects were found lying neatly out on someone's bed in plain view at a later time.

When psychics Ed and Lorraine Warren visited the house in the 1970s, the troubled spirit Lorraine sensed was not Molly, but a strong-willed, insecure woman she believed was Gen. Douglas MacArthur's mother. The Warrens believe they were able to help Mrs. MacArthur on her way to the light.

The bedding on a bunk in Colonel Thayer's private offices in the basement, which are always kept locked, had often been found tousled, as if someone had purposely thrown the blankets around. Lorraine sensed a "young and mischievous" spirit in that room, according to the in-house memorandums. That sounds more like an aide to the colonel than his fussy maid.

Lorraine also saw an apparition of an African American man dressed in an early 1900s uniform and stripped of all honors standing on the parade grounds outside the window. She said he was looking at the house sadly and told her his name was Greer. When she offered that she could tell he was troubled, he responded that he was "not free." Lorraine saw him in a small cell in her mind and said he seemed to be confined. When she asked what happened to him, he disappeared.

Superintendent Knowlton asked the West Point librarian to research the information he had provided that was gleaned from the Warrens' investigation and see if there was any historic evidence to back up Lorraine's impressions. In a disposition form dated November 3, 1972, found in the USMA Archives, a possible connection was discovered for the man named Greer. Prisoner Lawrence Greer was an African American private in Troop C, 9th Cavalry. The disposition states that Greer had "escaped from confinement at Fort Leavenworth" in 1931, but was captured near Albany the following spring and taken to West Point. There, he was court-martialed for desertion, found guilty, and sentenced to two-and-a-half years of hard labor. But the sentence was "disapproved by command of MG Connor," because Greer had been deemed insane at his trial. There are no records indicating what became of him after that. Was he then confined to a small cell in a mental institution? That would explain his sorrow and his words to

Lorraine. Was the guilt and shame he must have endured at West Point enough to keep his spirit trapped there long after his physical body had been buried?

Deathbed Deception

In the 1920s, a couple of servant girls who worked for a Captain Bellinger allegedly ran screaming half-naked from the Morrison House at 107B Washington Road, Professor's Row, claiming they had been chased out of the house by a female ghost. Bellinger was aware of the house's supernatural reputation prior to moving in, because stories had circulated that a woman who died there haunted her old room. He had no reason to believe it until then.

The house was built in 1821, the first house to go up on Professor's Row. It was named after one of its former residents, Col. William E. Morrison, professor of modern language from 1925 to 1948. By the time the Morrisons arrived, the place was already stigmatized, thanks to the well-publicized incident described above.

There are two rumors explaining why an unfriendly female apparition would haunt the rear, second-floor bedroom where the servant girls slept. One says she was a former occupant who loved the room so much that she refused to share it . . . and refused to leave it, even after death. The other says the ghost was a professor's wife who was furious about a promise her husband made on her deathbed that he broke shortly after she died; he swore he would never marry her mother. His mother-in-law!

A 1972 *New York Times* article said the woman died in the house and had been seen occasionally floating in through the window, according to a colonel who said the two servant girls were so terrified that they fled the building in "a state of relative undress." A priest was summoned to the residence to rid the house of any evil entities. After that, the girls were never bothered again.

Phantom Platoon

A 2005 West Point graduate tells of a paranormal experience that took place at the Staff Duty Office one night. The officer on duty thought he heard cadets goofing off on the parade field shortly after midnight, so he hurried out on the field to confront them and send them on their way. But what he saw was far different than what he expected. An entire platoon wearing old uniforms and carrying muskets was in formation, marching off into the fog.

The parade field is adjacent to a baseball stadium, Fort Clinton, and Clinton Field, as well as the Clinton parking lot that was once the site of numerous hangings of spies during the Revolutionary War. That function earned it monikers such as "Hangman's Walk," "Hangman's Gallows," "Hangman's Hollow," and "Gallows Hollow." The burial grounds for the hanged men were primarily where the division barracks are now located. (Hence, the possibility that Crusher in Room 4714 was a spirit whose grave was disturbed when the gravesites had to be relocated in 1820). Shortly after the remains were reinterred, a fire burned down the officer's quarters that were originally on the site, before the barracks were built. In 1894, a spontaneous combustion in the ice house at that same location was actually blamed on ghosts during a rash of other unexplainable incidents chronicled in the *New York Times*.

Eternal Obedience

In an incident somewhat similar to the above, Cadet Cpl. Theodore Hoham shared a story that was told to him by a professor not long ago:

> A few years ago, the Central Guard Room called the cadet first captain early in the morning to report that a cadet was outside his barracks marching in full uniform with a rifle in the dark. The first captain dressed himself and went out to confront the cadet, who snapped to attention and saluted, reporting his name and stating that he still owed several hours of disciplinary tours [given to cadets as punishment, they must march with a rifle for hours until their sentence has been served] before he was allowed to leave. He then disappeared. When the first captain looked up the cadet's name, he found that he had died when he still owed several hours on the area. The cadet was seen off and on for several months, but has since stopped coming around, presumably because he has paid his required time.

Now that's obedience. Hoham may have been joking when he quipped, "Most of us believe that the academy does, in fact, own our souls." But maybe he was closer to the truth than he realized.

The Good Catholic Ghost

On the West Point ghost tour, Shara McGowan, a 1993 USMA graduate, told of the haunted cemetery at the Most Holy Trinity Catholic Chapel.

Late one brisk night in the 1930s, a cadet was on his way to Mass when a man in a long black coat and top hat walking on the other side of the street beckoned him. The man was seeking directions to a certain section of the cemetery. The cadet crossed the street and told him as best he could how to get there, then returned to the other side of the road and continued on his way. A moment later, he realized he should have told the gentleman how to get there using a common shortcut, so he turned to call to the man, but the stranger was nowhere in sight. He couldn't possibly have moved that quickly. The cadet looked up and down the street and peered into the cemetery, which was lit by street lamps, but there was definitely no one around.

The cadet proceeded to Mass and then headed back to his room. After casually mentioning the stranger to his roommate, he learned that he had given directions to a well-known ghost who stops unsuspecting passersby at least once a year near the chapel asking for directions to a particular part of the cemetery.

Lower
Hudson Valley

THE LOWER HUDSON REGION COVERS WESTCHESTER, ROCKLAND, Putnam, and Bergen counties. This is the heart of Sleepy Hollow Country. Here is Washington Irving's haunted estate, Sunnyside, and a house in Nyack that forced a judge to declare, "As a matter of law, this house is haunted." There are also spirits in a mine, train depot, restaurant, castle, inn, and another mansion. Phantom cats prowl this land, which is also especially renowned for its mysterious stone chambers that dot the landscape in Putnam County.

The famous monolithic enigma Balanced Rock stands in North Salem. Some speculate that such stone structures are related to the UFO activity that has been long reported in the Brewster region. A major instance of visitation occurred in the winter of 1983. The sensational 1984 incident involving a massive UFO that hovered for fifteen minutes over the Indian Point 3 nuclear power plant in Buchanan has attained number one status on some top ten UFO sightings lists.

Ghost Legalese

Although the paranormal activity associated with the late Helen Ackley's house in Nyack was exceptional, what's even more unusual is what the sale of her property forced the New York State

Supreme Court to decide in 1991. Ackley could not legally deny the existence of ghosts in her house, because she had reported paranormal experiences to a national publication and to the local press right up until the year she put the house on sale. In the case *Stambovsky v. Ackley*, the justices determined by a majority vote "as a matter of law, the house is haunted." With that, the case was closed, but a big can of worms was opened. The real estate world would never be the same again.

Helen Ackley had long touted her house as being haunted, even submitting her story to *Readers Digest*, which featured an article about the house in its May 1977 issue. A local newspaper ran a story about the haunted property three times in the 1970s and 1980s. With Ackley's permission, the house was even included on a five-house ghost tour.

According to Ackley, who lived in the Victorian house at 1 LaVeta Place since the 1960s, several very noticeable spirits paid frequent visits to her home, but at least none were threatening. The ghosts woke up the late sleepers of the house by shaking their beds, and little gifts, like gold baby rings, seemed to materialize out of the blue on special occasions. Ackley and others claimed they had actually seen apparitions of several spirits over the years. One ghost reminded Ackley of jolly old Saint Nicholas. There was another who wore clothing from the Revolutionary War era and one who nodded his approval at her as she painted the living room one day. One female specter wore a hooded cloak. Footsteps were often heard in the stairway, cold spots were frequently felt, and the chandelier in the dining room occasionally swayed back and forth without explanation. All of the above were duly reported to the news media.

In 1990, Ackley decided to sell her famous, spirit-plagued home to an interested couple that was new to the area. She didn't mention the house's ghostly reputation to them, however. It wasn't until after Jeffrey and Patrice Stambovsky had given Ackley a hefty down payment for the $650,000 property that some neighbors told the couple the troubling news. The Stambovskys were not interested in living with ghosts or buying an expensive house with a tainted reputation that could diminish the property value. So they demanded to have the contract of sale rescinded and filed an action for damages because of fraudulent misrepresentation by both Ackley and the realtor. Eventually, the case made its way up to the state Supreme Court. The Stambovskys ultimately won by a three-to-two vote.

The case led to a ruling that property owners and real estate agents must divulge such information to potential buyers, if they are aware of such rumors. By the mid-1990s, there had been such a commotion over the ruling that "stigmatized property laws" were passed. These laws required real estate agents to only divulge known physical defects of a home or business; nothing intangible that may have stigmatized the property, such as crimes, murders, deaths, and paranormal activity. In other words, today in New York State the onus is once again on the buyer to determine prior to signing a contract of sale whether a house is haunted or not. That's not an easy thing to do, unless the seller allows you to bring in psychics and paranormal investigators for an overnight stay. Thanks to the original decision, however, many real estate agencies now require their agents to divulge whether they're aware of a home being haunted or not, if asked . . . just to be on the safe side.

Ackley sold the house in 1991 and moved to Florida. She passed away in 2003. The spirits she befriended apparently moved out when she did, because there have been no further reports of paranormal activity at 1 LaVeta Place since then.

Natural Wonder or Sacrificial Tomb?

The Balanced Rock at 667 Titicus Road in North Salem is an enigma. How did the massive, sixty-ton granite boulder come to rest precisely on five much smaller limestone "pillars" several millennia ago? The geological anomaly looks like a precarious arrangement of nature, but so do all ancient dolmens. A "dolmen," or portal tomb, is a type of megalith believed to be a Neolithic tomb, fashioned by balancing one very large capstone on top of two or more smaller, upright stones. These are found all over Europe, Africa, and the British Isles, but not so much in the United States, although there are a couple of similar balanced rocks in New Hampshire.

Some scientists insist that the Balanced Rock is a glacial creation—the North Salem Historical Society once even identified the landmark with a sign saying it had been pushed there during the Ice Age more than ten thousand years ago. Today many people are leaning toward the theory that it was manmade. In keeping with that modern school of thought, the marker now offers both theories:

> The Balanced Rock is estimated to weigh 60 tons. Geologists refer to it as "an erratic." The boulder is composed of granite that does not match rocks normally found in this vicinity and is thought to have been deposited here during the glacial period. It has been suggested in recent years that this may be a dolmen, a Celtic ceremonial stone used to memorialize its dead.

There is a third theory about the boulder formation in North Salem. Some believe it may be related to UFO sightings, which have historically been plentiful in that vicinity, with its close proximity to Brewster, Reservoir Road, and the Upper and Lower Magnetic Mine Road mentioned in other stories in this book. In fact, Titicus Road, on Routes 116 and 121, has had plenty of its own UFO and alien sightings. Elusive cloaked figures have been seen near the stone, and there have been several reports that a triangular UFO has been observed hovering over the boulder and beaming a white light directly down on it.

When authorities dismissed the reports, saying it was just helicopters patrolling the area, witnesses responded that the UFOs they saw were silent, unlike any helicopter they had ever heard. Photographs taken at the site frequently reveal orbs and other light anomalies, even if they weren't seen with the naked eye.

Many people who visit the site have experienced headaches and nausea, as well as sinus pressure in their heads. This may be due to the magnetic deviations known to exist in the environment, near the magnetic mines. But others believe that some individuals are more sensitive to whatever took place thousands of years ago at that boulder and are unconsciously tapping into the emotions related to past incidents. The Balanced Rock, regardless of what it is and where it came from, is now listed in several sources as one of the "Sacred Power Sites" in the United States.

Emily's Room

Does Emily Roebling haunt the Bird and Bottle Inn at 1123 Old Albany Post Road in the hamlet of Garrison? Paranormal activity occurring in or near the bedroom that was once hers makes many suspect she does.

Emily was born on September 23, 1843, to Sylvanus and Phoebe Warren in nearby Cold Spring. In 1865, she married Washington Roebling, son of Brooklyn Bridge designer John A. Roebling and later chief engineer of the monumental construction of the bridge.

When Washington became disabled by decompression sickness from working in compressed air under the river in the latter stages of the thirteen-year job, Emily became her husband's spokesperson and virtually took over the engineering feat. An astute child, Emily had always had an unusual affinity for math and science, especially for a young woman of that time. As fate would have it, that passion enabled her to carry on when her husband could no longer visit the job site and supervise the job. Emily learned civil engineering and helped guide the massive project to fruition, primarily under her direction. She earned the right to be the first female ever to cross the Brooklyn Bridge.

The Roeblings lived in Trenton, New Jersey, but when their only child attended college at Rensselaer Polytechnic Institute (RPI) in Troy, they returned to the Hudson Valley for four years to be near him. In 1903, after a lifetime of devotion to her family and community, sixty-year-old Emily succumbed to stomach cancer and muscular atrophy at her home in Trenton.

Emily's parents owned and operated Warren's Tavern as a stagecoach stop catering to those traveling between Albany and New York City. Though the Warrens called the inn home in the mid-1800s, it had actually been built in 1761, making it one of the oldest inns in New York State. In 1832, before the Warrens purchased the property, it had been a farm with a saw and gristmill.

In 1940, Warren's Tavern became the Bird and Bottle Inn. Today, its first floor houses one of finest formal restaurants in the Hudson Valley. The second floor offers three restored guestrooms, including Emily's Room, with antique furnishings and fireplaces complementing the original, wide-plank wood floors. Here, history seems to come alive, in more ways than one.

Co-owner Elaine Margolies told a reporter for the *New York Times* in 2007 that their ghost stories are not frightening, but instead rather humorous. Footsteps are heard on the stairs nearby and objects become "unaccountably displaced." Unexplained banging is heard on pipes, and champagne bottles are found opened. Emily's childhood room is said to be haunted by a good-natured ghost, and although the spirit is believed to be Emily, the room has belonged to many people both before and after her.

Brewster, the Other UFO Hotspot

To the west of the Hudson River lies the famous Pine Bush UFO hotspot, but the region east of the Hudson River will not be outdone, according to Search Project for Aspects of Close Encounters (SPACE). The village of Brewster is the Hudson Valley's other UFO hotspot. Roughly five thousand people reported seeing giant, dark, and slow-moving boomerang aerial objects in the skies over the area during a four-year period in the 1980s.

The winter of 1983 was particularly memorable for some of Brewster residents. On February 26, a self-described "level-headed" employee of the town was driving home from dinner with her teenage daughter, when the latter pointed to a huge, two-hundred-foot, triangular object with about fifty multicolored lights that was skimming the tree line, about thirty feet off the ground and moving at the same slow speed as their car. It then hovered, as if it were as curious about the two gawking humans as they were about the strange flying object. After about ten minutes, it slowly moved on, only to startle a dozen more residents who reported the same thing, but from different locations in the tiny town.

The following month, on the evening of St. Patrick's Day, another young mother looked out of her window toward I-84 and was shocked to see a large, V-shaped object with countless bright lights of every color hovering over a truck that had pulled off the highway. Hudson Valley residents are no strangers to UFO reports, so she wasn't afraid, only curious. She opened the window to listen, but the object, which was slowly drifting toward her house, made no sound at all. It then made a very precise ninety-degree turn toward her neighbor's house, and she watched in amazement as her neighbor stood in his garden directly beneath the object, bathed in its spotlight. The woman looked away from the spectacle long enough to call to her husband. Many others witnessed the same event. Traffic had come to a standstill on the interstate, as cars, including a state police cruiser, pulled off the highway to watch. Then, as slowly and silently as it had arrived, the dark, metallic craft, estimated to be the size of a football field, moved off toward the north and out of sight.

Magnetic Mine Road is rife with supernatural phenomena and has intrigued ufologists for years. Some have speculated that the abandoned mines and mysterious stone chambers in the vicinity may be used as secret alien bases because of the heavy UFO traffic near those structures. Likewise, it's believed that so many helicopters and military aircraft fly over the region at all hours of the night in order to keep an eye on the extraterrestrials.

In 1988, a couple parked on Upper Magnetic Mine Road (Reservoir Road) to see what all the talk was about. It was just past midnight when they noticed several figures in the distance that seemed to be floating single-file through the woods. The beings moved fluidly, almost like ghosts, but they had oversized, bald heads and glowing green eyes.

In 1991, several people saw a UFO actually land on Upper Magnetic Mine Road and watched as several forms left the saucer-shaped spacecraft, scurried across the road, and morphed into more human-like forms, but with hooded robes and no discernible faces. Another member of the group who was waiting in the car saw three "grays," archetypal aliens, approach the vehicle from behind, moving in a freakish lockstep manner. Her screams prompted the menacing figures to instantly disappear. Meanwhile the faceless, robed figures slanted impossibly to the ground when another vehicle approached, only to reappear upright moments later in the trees, without having missed a beat. Also on Upper Magnetic Mine Road, a very petite, feminine form illuminated by a greenish glow has been spotted. The figure reportedly gives off a gentle, benevolent, magical energy when encountered. People who have seen her say the sense of peacefulness she fills them with lasts for months afterward.

Two Minutes Too Late

In 1898, a wealthy Cold Spring woman overheard her husband talking about his plans to have her killed. Horrified, she sneaked out of their house and fled down Main Street, literally running for her life. The only thing she could think of doing on a moment's notice like that was to take the 10:15 P.M. train to the Poughkeepsie station and get to her brother's house as quickly as possible. He would protect her. But even as she raced to the train station, her husband had already noticed her missing and set out at once to search the village for her. Realizing that she must have heard his conversation, he knew he had to get to her before she could get to someone else and incriminate him.

Cold Spring Depot, in the Hudson Highlands village of the same name, is now a historic landmark and a popular family restaurant and bar owned by Tom Rolston. Located at the foot of Main Street at 1 Depot Square, the old train station is in close proximity to the Metro North platform. The original ticket office is now the bar area, and the walls are adorned with artwork depicting actual scenes and people from the station's heyday. In the winter, the cozy fireside dining in the original depot waiting room draws people in, and in the summer, the allure of outdoor seating likewise attracts customers seeking year-round comfort food.

Built in 1893 by Cornelius Vanderbilt, the storied train depot sits on property where George Washington once allegedly drank from the spring. Originally, the depot served as both a passenger and a freight terminal and was very active as such until 1954. Then it was sold and turned into a Jeep dealership for a time. It wasn't until 1972 that it became a restaurant, and in 1986, an outdoor park was added. Today, you can sit on the patio outside of the restaurant and watch roughly sixty-eight trains go through on any given day— that's about one train every ten to fifteen minutes. They pass by the old station fast and frequently. But on that winter's evening in 1898, the 10:15 arrived two minutes too late for an ill-fated wife. Her homicidal husband reached the station faster on foot than the next train to Poughkeepsie.

As she sat on the waiting bench, trembling more from fear than the cold of the air, she barely had time to turn when her deranged husband pounced upon her. Without so much as a pause, he grabbed her with one hand, pulled a knife out of his pocket with the other, and thrust it deep into her chest. She died instantly. But if he thought he would get away with murder, he was dead wrong. The public was outraged by the senseless killing and he was arrested, convicted of murder, and hanged for his crime.

Some say the woman now haunts the Cold Spring Depot, perhaps because her death was so sudden and unexpected that it left her in a confused state, unable to accept that her escape was foiled and her life cut short. They say that on Wednesday nights at precisely 10:13 P.M., a cold chill is felt on the very spot where she died.

To My Daughter, I Leave . . .

Estherwood Mansion at 49 Clinton Avenue in Dobbs Ferry is said to be one of the most haunted of the ritzy houses along the Hudson River. It may also be the most scandal-plagued. The lavish, three-and-a-half-story manor rests on a ten-acre plot just east of the main buildings of the Masters School, a private, coeducational, boarding school. It was built between 1894 and 1895 by industrialist James Jenning McComb and his wife Esther Wood McComb, for whom the mansion is named. The McCombs' three daughters, Mary, Fanny, and Lilly, attended when it was still an all-girls school, and the family, which also included son Jennings, lived there for six years until James died at the residence on March 31, 1901. The *New York Times* said he died from a "complication of diseases resulting from kidney trouble." He had been critically ill for several weeks and unwell for months prior to his passing.

McComb's last will and testament held some surprises for his heirs. The wealthy patriarch, whose estate was valued at around $15 million, was generous and judicious in providing for his siblings and their children, as well as others who were not blood relatives. To his beloved wife and four children, he left the Estherwood estate. He also left Esther their well-located New York City residence, along with $30,000 toward Dobbs Ferry expenses and a $412,000 income for personal use. To his children he left an annual income of $6,000 and a one-fourth share of Estherwood upon their mother's death. Here's where it gets interesting. The father apparently didn't approve of his daughter Fannie's choice of a suitor, a well-known Philadelphia artist named Louis Herzog. According to the *New York Times*, dated April 23, 1901, Fannie would be disinherited if she were to marry Herzog.

> In regard to the paragraph in the codicil which referred to the provision for the daughter, Miss Fannie . . . she would be better off if she did not [marry Herzog]. By the provisions of the will, she was left an annuity of $6,000 and a one-fourth share in the residuary estate on the death of her mother. By a codicil the testator provided that, if she married Mr. Herzog, she could receive only $15,000, and that only on condition that he does not interfere with her enjoyment of it. By not marrying him, she will come, in due time, into about $5,000,000.

Estherwood was valued at $15 million, and Fannie would lose her quarter share in it if she married Herzog. This created a flurry of excitement in the news media and within the family circle. The palpable tension in her family, coupled with the stress of losing her husband, proved too much for the elderly Esther. On July 2, 1901, just three months after her husband died in that very home, she died at Estherwood as well, and the prized estate passed to the children.

Several months later, Fannie contested her father's will, determined to find a way to both marry Herzog and acquire her fair share of the family estate. The judge ruled that no decision would be made until she actually wed Herzog. So Fannie and Louis were married in 1901 on New Year's Eve. On March 24, 1903, according to the *New York Times*, a Supreme Court justice announced the decision that "Mrs. Fannie Rayne McComb Herzog will not suffer the loss of one cent." She won her case.

Later that year, things turned even more bizarre. The husband of Fannie's sister Lillie, Granville W. Garth, disappeared mysteriously at sea on Christmas night, while en route to Galveston, Texas, for health reasons (he suffered from a severe state of mental depression). Garth was a banker and one of the executors of James McComb's estate. Family and friends claimed they had placed Garth in the care of a Mr. Lawson, with whom he worked. Lawson denied responsibility for the disappearance and suggested that Garth had jumped or fallen overboard and that the ship's crew should have been watching him better.

The missing man, it was pointed out in news articles, had recently come into wealth from the will of McComb through his wife Lillie. There were rumors that "domestic difficulties" had led to his troubled state of mind. It would later be revealed that Lillie secretly purchased a beautiful home in Morristown, New Jersey, less than two weeks before her husband's suspicious disappearance. The deed, however, was still not filed with the county clerk three months later on April 8, 1904. It was also well known that Lillie agreed that Fannie should receive her fair share of the estate, regardless of her father's wishes. According to a *Times* article on December 30, 1903:

> Neither Mrs. Garth, nor her brother-in-law, Louis Herzog, would discuss last night the latest explanation provided by Andrew A. Knowles, cashier of the Mechanics' National Bank, of the causes of "illness" of Granville W. Garth, supposed to have been drowned in the Gulf of Mexico. Mr. Knowles declared that "it will be found that Mr. Garth died the victim of Southern chivalry, trying to shield the good name of his family."

The very next day, two years to the date of her forbidden marriage, Fannie filed a petition to have Garth replaced as the McComb estate executor. She also demanded a compulsory accounting of the estate.

In 1910, the Masters School purchased the estate, along with adjacent properties McComb had acquired in his seven years there. Not much has been altered, except for an elevator that was added in 1949. The building, which served as a dormitory for many years, has been meticulously maintained. Today, the main floor, with its stunning grand staircase and stained glass ceilings, is regularly rented out for special events. Nine apartments on the second floor and third floor provide rent-free faculty housing. Mystery dinner theaters have also been held there. And the mansion houses one or more ghosts.

Some people believe the ghost of a young lady who lived at Estherwood while it was a dormitory is there. Others attribute paranormal activity to a woman who supposedly hanged herself after learning of her husband's infidelity. The house may also be unsettled because of the events surrounding McComb's will. Has the lost executor Granville Garth returned? Or perhaps the complete disregard of a patriarch's wishes has roused troubled McComb spirits in the house.

The Spaceship and the Power Plant

On June 11, 1984, police officers saw six lights flying in a V formation over the New Castle town hall. That same month, similar sightings were reported over Briarcliff Manor, Peekskill, and Katonah. Following this, a series of sightings began at the state-run Indian Point 3 (IP3) nuclear power plant in Buchanan. The first incident occurred on June 14, when three project security personnel saw a giant aircraft unlike anything they had ever seen before doing a brief flyover of the nuclear facility.

Then on the evening of July 24, a dozen IP3 security guards reportedly looked up to see a massive ship, with six to ten white lights outlining its boomerang shape, hovering over the power plant.

The guards would get a better look ten days later when the object reappeared; one of the twelve guards that saw it blurted out its arrival over the plant's paging system. Another guard allegedly got a rooftop view of the belly of the object and pulled his gun instinctively on it when it moved a bit, but he didn't shoot. All of the guards stood gaping at the object overhead, prepared to execute an order to shoot it down should one come. On the surveillance monitor inside the facility, stunned guards watched the object. They described it as larger than a football field with eight bright lights in a V shape. It hovered over the exhaust tower of the reactor for fifteen minutes, long enough for everyone, including ten of the nearby Consolidated Edison security personnel, to get a good look. All agreed on the shape of the light formation outlining the object. The only thing they couldn't agree on was whether its intentions were threatening or just curiosity.

A Brewster businessman captured ten minutes of video footage of what is believed to be the same object as it passed over town just fifteen minutes before its shocking visit to IP3. According to various news reports and a 1987 book about the incident, at least seventy plant personnel saw the object. Government agencies, including officials of IP3, say that the large, hovering object that parked itself

directly over the nuclear reactor was merely a peculiar formation of planes playing tricks on the eyes of the beholders. Obviously others believe the mysterious object was from another world.

Today, the Indian Point Energy Center is operated by Entergy Nuclear Northeast. IP3 remains active and has applied to have its operating license extended by twenty years. The mysterious UFO has not returned.

Never to Leave

It wasn't hard to determine who haunts Dr. Martha MacGuffie's medieval-style stone castle at 591 South Mountain Road in New City. The apparition of a six-and-a-half-foot-tall man with long, silver hair could only be Harold Deming, the lawyer who built the house in the 1930s. He loved his property and the massive house he modeled after a thirteenth-century Norman castle. He often quipped he would never leave it. When he died of a sudden heart attack on his estate ten years after the castle was built, the words on his tombstone reflected that sentiment: "From this place I shall never roam." His gravesite is on the grounds.

Dr. MacGuffie, cofounder of the nonprofit Society for Hospital and Resource Exchange (SHARE), which benefits the children of Africa, runs a plastic and reconstructive surgery practice on the first level of the mansion she purchased in 1949. Originally, that area was an open porch and a large wine cellar. Today it consists of offices and exam rooms . . . and heavy doors that refuse to stay shut, opening inexplicably. Footsteps can be heard walking across empty rooms and up and down the hallways. Is it Deming, as many believe?

A few months after the family moved into the house, Dr. MacGuffie's housekeeper, Eliza Henry, encountered the lanky, long-haired gentleman in a long hallway on the second floor. He was later identified as Deming by his daughters, based on Eliza's description. The housekeeper saw the same distinct apparition several times, prompting her to confess to the doctor that the only thing she didn't love about the beautiful house was "that man," the spirit. He always stood in the same spot at the end of the hall, staring out the window in quiet contemplation, seemingly unaware that he was being watched by the housekeeper. Ironically, Eliza died in that very hallway at the age of fifty-nine.

Deming's daughter also told Dr. MacGuffie about her father's daily routine, which apparently included leaving the house via the back door early each day to navigate the entire circumference of his property before returning to the rear entrance where he had begun. He did this faithfully day after day. Strangely, long after Deming's death, one of Dr. MacGuffie's cats began to exhibit the exact same compulsion on a daily basis, as if it were following in the deceased's footsteps.

There is nothing to fear about the peaceful, benevolent presence that cohabits with Dr. MacGuffie in her home and office. The doctor has put the building's reputation to good use, hosting a haunted castle event, with the proceeds going to her charity, SHARE.

Alien Big Cats

Like the dreaded black dogs of British lore, whose appearance near cemeteries is said to precede death, black cats have been long associated with the supernatural. After all, the color black in many cultures symbolizes death and evil, and cats have always been inherently mysterious creatures, regardless of color. In the folk culture of many European countries since the Middle Ages, black cats have been related to misfortune.

Early European settlers in America brought their superstitions to the colonies, where black felines were said to be manifestations of the devil or the familiars of witches. Like alleged witches, black cats were sometimes hunted down and burned or drowned, especially on religious holidays like Easter. Today, of course, cats of all colors and breeds have become the world's most popular pet, but if a large, mysterious black cat crossed your path out of nowhere and just stood there staring at you, wouldn't you find it a little unnerving?

In July 2009, a father and son were enjoying a leisurely bike ride in Rockland County's Tallman Mountain State Park when they came upon two huge black cats, the size of jaguars, in the woods. That's something you don't see every day in the Hudson Valley. The animals didn't seem to notice them, even when the two hurried away. The father found the park rangers and described the size of the cats and said they had glossy black fur and three-foot-long tails. The rangers accompanied the father and son back to the scene, where several huge paw prints remained, but the cats were nowhere to be found.

This was not the first big cat sighting in the area. A woman recently spotted similar big cats on the Palisades Parkway. None of this would be overly alarming were jaguars native to the region. The black panther, a tag generically given to the growing pool of unidentified large black cats found outside of their natural habitat, has been sporadically reported in warmer climates like Kentucky and the Carolinas, but rarely are these creatures seen so far north.

Some people speculate the cats may have been former pets that escaped or were released into the wild. Others, like cryptozoologists, believe they could represent the enigmatic "phantom cats," also known as "Alien Big Cats" or "ABCs," referring to cats not indigenous to the area in which they were seen. Cryptozoology, the study of "hidden animals" that scientists don't necessarily believe exist, also concentrates on identifying wild animals outside of their normal geographic ranges. Scientists insist that such animals don't live in the Hudson Valley or in any other North Country region and say they are likely bear cubs or bobcats that are misidentified by the witnesses.

Wildlife agencies tend to have a healthy skepticism, but suggest that exotic animals do sometimes stray far from their natural environments. As a precaution, state police dispatched additional staff to Tallman Mountain to see if they could shed some light on the enigma.

What's That Sound?

Shortly after midnight on Saturday, March 7, 2009, a loud, mysterious "boom" rattled windows throughout Westchester County, prompting calls to police stations and news media outlets in Eastchester, Bronxville, and Yonkers. It was not weather-related, according to meteorologists, although it sounded like a tremendous crash of thunder. It was not a sonic boom from aircraft breaking the sound barrier, according to airport officials. It was also found to be neither fireworks nor a gas explosion, according to area utilities and emergency responders, nor was it a blown power transformer, according to power plant officials. So what was it? One Mount Kisco resident happened to be looking out her window at precisely the time the boom was heard. She saw a bright yellow object streaking across the sky at exactly the same moment.

Early the following Monday morning, a similar blast awakened Rockland County residents across the Hudson River. Again, no source was found for the sound. If that wasn't unusual enough, exactly one week later on March 16, 2009, Staten Island residents just thirty-four miles south of the Hudson River Valley reported their own loud boom just before 8:00 P.M. in at least six neighborhoods of the borough. Once again, although the usual theories were offered, each one was categorically dispelled, with the exception of a possible meteor breaking the sound barrier as it fell toward the earth's surface. In that case, there may be three or four meteorites out there, somewhere in the Hudson Valley and Staten Island, and they may be worth a small fortune.

Much to her surprise, one woman was rewarded in 1992, when a meteorite tore right through her car's trunk as the vehicle sat unoccupied in her driveway in Peekskill. Michelle Knapp received $50,000 for the meteorite, and the totaled red Malibu coupe, dubbed the "Peekskill Meteorite Car," was purchased from her and put on world tour. The incident is considered to be the most publicized meteoric event of modern times.

It's rare enough to have just one meteorite reveal itself by means of a mysterious boom heard for miles around, but to hear three or four booms in the same general vicinity in the course of just ten days seems extraordinary. No source was ever found for any of the booms.

The Stone Chambers

Putnam County's stone chambers are as baffling today as they were during colonial times, when area clergy warned Hudson Valley residents to stay away from them, thinking they were portals to hell. They likened them to Druid-built stone chambers in Ireland. That ancient, mystical religion, little understood as it was at the time, was considered evil. With more than two hundred such chambers—and forty-six in the town of Kent alone—that's an awful lot of hellholes in a relatively small area. Putnam County, in fact, has the most stone chambers in the Northeast, and along with two other counties in New England, the three areas account for the majority of stone chambers in all of America.

By the early 1800s, sensibility prevailed over superstition, and farmers began using some of the chambers as storage space. They may have even been so impressed with the sturdy stone structures that they attempted to build replicas. Nevertheless, there are those who insist that the chambers were all built in the eighteenth and nineteenth centuries by farmers to use as root cellars, manmade "refrigerators" carved into the ground or hillside using stone, mortar, wood, and sod. The Putnam County chambers, however, are made entirely of stone, using no mortar, wood, or sod, and are nearly twice as large as the typical root cellar.

Nobody has studied the stone chambers more thoroughly from a paranormal standpoint than researcher and author Phillip Imbrogno. In 2008, he penned an article called "UFOs and the Stone Chambers of New York's Hudson Valley" for the *Alien Seeker News* online, which laid out theories that most historians and archaeologists have shunned. He believes the chambers were built around 1000 B.C. by Celtic explorers and that they have since been used by ancient Indian tribes and perhaps, even now, by extraterrestrials. Imbrogno has devoted a tremendous amount of time seeking expert opinion and researching historical documents related to the stone chambers, as well as doing on-site investigations using compasses, magnetometers, and other applicable equipment.

Imbrogno said that every chamber he has studied was built over the top of two specific minerals, quartzite and magnetite, and most of them were built over underground water sources. So there seemed to be scientific reasoning behind the placement of the bunkers. Compass readings taken at each site were off by 5 to 180 degrees. Magnetic field readings at every site produced negative results on the magnetometer. Imbrogno said the strength of magnetic deviation implies that the natural magnetic field was being pulled as if into a vortex, where the magnetism was reduced or even obliterated. What could cause such a reaction? A physicist told him that such a huge magnetic anomaly theoretically could be caused by "a large spherical mass, twelve feet or larger, composed of high grade iron" buried up to ten feet below the chamber. Sounds like what some people have been seeing in the skies over Putnam

County and the entire Hudson Valley for years, which brings us to the next theory—the ancient chambers were made instead by aliens who carefully buried their spaceships beneath them. That would certainly explain the UFO sightings and alien encounters that are so prevalent around the chambers.

Supporters of the Druid theory point out the glyphics discovered on or within the stone chambers that are believed to be Ogham, a pictographic alphabet used by the Celts more than two thousand years ago. Imbrogno said that when the symbols found in the older chambers were transcribed by experts, it was determined that they were prayers to Celtic gods in honor of particular holidays or festivals. One professor estimated the age of the chambers to be about three thousand years based on the language etched into the stone. This was confirmed by Imbrogno, who used a program at the observatory where he worked at the time to determine the year of the planetary alignments that matched an astronomical conjunction etched into the exterior of one chamber. The fact that many of the carvings reflect astronomical themes and that the placement of the entrance and angle of the chambers serves as an ancient calendar marking the solstice can be attributed to Druids . . . and perhaps their association with aliens.

Another theory suggests that the chambers were sacred temples used by Native Americans whose medicine men communed with the Great Spirit from within the chambers. The chambers also have been called Indian burial tombs. Still others believe they were built by Vikings. So many theories and so few answers.

The Spirits of Smalley's Inn

The Smalley's Inn property on Route 52 in Carmel has been inhabited since the days of the Revolutionary War, when Elder Nathan Cole first owned it. It was one of only three village houses there. After Cole's death, Stephen Waring purchased the house to serve as both his residence and a store. The homestead was demolished in 1833, and a hotel was built on its foundation by Col. Thomas Taylor. Taylor and the hotel are noted in William S. Pelletreau's 1886 *History of Putnam County*:

During his life he was a well known and prominent citizen, and was elected member of the Legislature, and held the office of sheriff. He died August 1st, 1865, at the age of eighty. After his death, [the hotel] was purchased by James J. Smalley, from whom it derived its present name.

Some recent sources indicate that Smalley took over the property in 1852, and it then became known as the Smalley House and Smalley's Hotel. Smalley's death in 1867 forced the sale of the property to John Cornish, but the Smalley name is the one that remains associated with the property, likely because of his standing in the community.

Like Colonel Taylor, Smalley was a jack-of-all-trades—a two-time assemblyman, county sheriff, county treasurer, and county coroner. The latter job lead to rumors that a portion of the Smalley's Inn basement posed as a morgue during the family's stay there. In 1890, when the hotel also had a small store and bank in it, at least three engineers died unexpectedly while lodging at the Smalley Hotel, according to the *New York Times* of November 9, 1890:

> Carmel has proved rather an unfortunate place for civil engineers of the higher grades. No less than three assistant engineers of the Department of Public Works have died at the Smalley House, and yet the engineers who go to Carmel continue almost invariably to put up at the same hotel. This would indicate either that it is a very good house or else that engineers as a class are not superstitious.

Aside from the engineers and several previous owners who have passed away at Smalley's Inn, James Smalley's young daughter, Elizabeth, is thought to have died here as well. Some people believe she haunts the inn, manifesting as a little girl wearing what the owner calls "her *Little House on the Prairie* outfit." Some visitors say she tugs at their clothing. Anthony "Tony" Porto Jr. and his father now own Smalley's, but it has been in the Porto family since the 1950s, when Anthony Sr.'s mother purchased it. They run a charming Italian-American family restaurant in the building. Tony Jr. has seen Elizabeth, and his wife has heard a child giggling right beside her.

No records have been found indicating where Elizabeth actually died, but her tombstone was kept at Smalley's for a while after it

was dug up by a man who was building a house in town. Although the Portos no longer have the tombstone, the little girl's spirit reportedly ran around laughing playfully while the stone was there.

Apparitions of a man and a woman have also been seen by a number of people. Enough men have died at the hotel for it to be any of them. The female apparition is anyone's guess. Sporadic, unexplained incidents, such as slamming doors, footsteps, and a vacuum cleaner with a mind of its own, have occurred all over the property, from the upstairs apartment to the kitchen and basement. One incident stands out from all the others, however.

According to an October 2007 *Times Herald-Record* article, a strange thing happened one night at 10:33. Every phone in the building, including the cell phones, began calling the other lines in the building, one after the other. All the phones rang simultaneously, yet no one touched the dials!

Smalley's Inn was resurrected under the same name twice, after devastating fires in 1924 and 1974 destroyed the building. Though some current online sources say the fires were deadly, no actual lives were lost in either blaze according to old newspaper accounts published at the time. So the fires can't be blamed for the hauntings. The Portos believe a Ouija board that was used in the 1980s at Smalley's might be responsible. The board told Porto that nine people "wanted to play." That was when the sightings and paranormal incidents began. Whether the ghosts are the ill-fated engineers, former owners, little Elizabeth, or unknown entities who arrived via the Ouija board, their presence hasn't hurt business at Smalley's Inn and Restaurant at all.

Spook Rock

According to legend, a penny-pinching Dutch farmer who traded with the Lenape Indians was thought to have conned them one day. To get even, the Lenapes kidnapped his beautiful, young daughter and laid her out on top of their ceremonial rock, now called Spook Rock. There they allegedly slaughtered the innocent girl, following a sacrificial ceremony to teach the man who had wronged them a lesson. As the fair victim exhaled her last breath, her angry spirit arose defiantly from its brutalized body, right in front of the chief and his tribe, to their horror.

Ghost investigator and author Linda Zimmerman says that just after the murder, the Indian chief found out that the poor Dutch farmer had not conned them after all. The chief was haunted for the rest of his life, not only by his own guilt but also by the object of his guilt, the unhappy spirit of the child he had killed. While every member of the tribe saw her ghost hovering over the rock immediately after the deed was committed, sources vary on whether it was then seen by each person who had been present that day every night for the rest of their lives, or whether the tribe members continued to see it only on the eve of the anniversary of her death. Even today, scattered reports tell of an indistinct figure sometimes seen floating over Spook Rock, located at Spook Rock Road (County Route 85) and Highview Avenue (County Route 64) in the town of Tallman.

Some people have questioned the validity of this legend, saying local Indians did not believe in human sacrifice at that time. Others claim the story is a fair depiction of the tensions that sometimes existed between the Indians and the early Dutch settlers of the region. True or not, the legend has endured and will likely remain embedded in the fabric of Rockland County's historical tapestry.

Spook Rock Road has other legends associated with it as well. One tells of a young Dutch woman whose frequent trysts with her Indian lover at Spook Rock incensed the community, because they didn't approve of the courtship. So the Dutch settlers climbed the rock, taking the lovers by surprise one moonlit night, and murdered them right there on the spot. They say that the couple's screams can still be heard in the woods along the road today. A different version of that story has the tribe's god dealing the amorous couple his own brand of punishment by causing a flood to sweep them off the rock and into a pile of boulders downstream, where the two bodies came to rest at different locations. The woman is believed to still haunt the area with her sorrowful moans, searching for her long-lost lover.

Another tale tells of a devil-worshipping nun who was believed to have murdered a baby, until it was revealed that the father had actually done the horrible deed—and now both father and baby haunt an old mansion on the road.

Finally, there's the legend of Spook Rock Road that involves a phenomenon called "gravity hill." Though recent alterations to the road have reduced the number of reports, they say that if you put your car in neutral with the brakes off at the bottom of the hill leading to Spook Rock, it would appear to defy gravity and go backwards up the hill, as if being sucked back toward the haunted Spook Rock. This phenomenon is actually an optical illusion in which the lay of the land and its surroundings cause a very slight downward slope on the road to appear to actually be going uphill when it's not. There are hundreds of such hills around the world, but this one in the Hudson Valley just happens to be on a road appropriately named for such things.

When Will This End?

Washington Irving was one of America's most beloved and renowned authors of the nineteenth century. He was a great essayist, biographer, historian, and writer's advocate who fought for better copyright laws and encouraged the likes of Edgar Allan Poe and Nathaniel Hawthorne. In 1819, when his *The Sketch Book of Geoffrey Crayon, Gent* was published, Irving became a literary sensation nationally and internationally. Two of the most famous stories in *The Sketch Book*, "The Legend of Sleepy Hollow" and "Rip Van Winkle," have become synonymous with the enchanting, haunting Hudson Valley region.

Set in the Tarrytown of 1790, "Sleepy Hollow" gave us such characters as the dubious Brom Bones, the lovely Katrina Van Tassel, the unlucky-in-love Ichabod Crane, and, of course, the ghost of a headless horseman believed to be a Hessian soldier whose head was shot off by a stray cannonball during the Revolutionary War.

Irving himself was introduced to a ghost. When he moved into the small, two-room Dutch cottage known in 1835 as "Wolfert's Roost," Wolfert Acker's ghost allegedly haunted the apple orchard. Irving learned that the cottage had been built by the Van Tassel family in 1656, which intrigued the historian in him. He said of his new residence, "It is a beautiful spot, capable of being made a little paradise." Indeed, he spent many happy years expanding and remodeling the stone house, finally adding a tower that he called the Pagoda and renaming the picturesque dwelling Sunnyside.

Irving died at the age of seventy-six in his bedroom at Sunnyside on November 28, 1859. A *New York Times* article, "Washington Irving: Commemoration of the Birth and Death of the Great Historian," on April 4, 1860, told of his last moments:

> On the 28th of November last, in the evening, he had bidden the family good night in his usual kind manner, and had withdrawn to his room, attended by one of his nieces carrying his medicines, when he complained of a sudden feeling of intense sadness, sank immediately into her arms, and died without a struggle.

Legend has it that these were his last words: "Well, I must arrange my pillows for another night. When will this end?" Although he may have been ready to go after a life lived long and well, the nation mourned his passing, for his popularity was still rising even as he reached the twilight of his years.

A few years after his death, three people watched as Irving's spirit walked through the parlor of Sunnyside, disappearing into the library. Located on West Sunnyside Lane off Route 9 in Irvington, Sunnyside remained in the Irving family until 1945, when they sold it to John D. Rockefeller Jr., who opened it to the public two years later. In 1962, it became a National Historic Landmark, and today it is operated as a museum by Historic Hudson Valley.

There are reports that the spirits of Irving's nieces, who doted on their uncle, have been known to tidy things up in the middle of the night, much to the delight of staff opening up the next day. Washington Irving obviously loved a good ghost story, and it was no secret how much he loved his Sunnyside estate. By haunting Sunnyside, he can still enjoy both.

Not for Naut

At the southwest corner of Strawtown and Germonds roads in the hamlet of West Nyack, formerly Clarksville, lie the ruins of an old gristmill where the last witchcraft trial in New York State purportedly took place. Being the widow of a Scottish physician, Jane Kannif, whom the Clarksville people called "Naut," was familiar with folk remedies made with herbs that were native to the Hudson Valley. Armed with this knowledge, she was often called upon by her neighbors to hasten their recovery from various ailments. Naut had moved into Clarksville with her only child, Tobia Lowrie. But in

1816, the oddly-dressed, peculiar woman with a knack for healing was rumored to be a witch by some in her community when children living nearby became plagued by hives and butter was said to stop churning. Someone had to be blamed, and this woman who was so different became their prime target.

Naut was taken from her New City Road home and dragged across the road to a mill pond to be dunked. The dunking ritual was a means of determining who was a witch. Naut's hands and feet would be bound, and she would be tossed into a deep body of water. If she drowned, she was innocent; if she did not sink and drown, she would be labeled a witch. That meant she would have to be burned at the stake, hanged, or crushed under a pile of stones. So she would be damned if she did and damned if she didn't.

According to the story as told by Keith P. Graham on his blog *Wanderings*, just as the people were about to toss Naut into the pond, bound hand and foot, some men convinced them to use a different means of divining the truth—the old weigh-the-witch trick. They carried poor Naut to the Polhemus Grist Mill and placed her onto a large flour scale opposite a heavy, wood-and brass-bound Holland Dutch Bible to see which weighed more. If a suspected witch weighed less than a Bible, then she was a witch. Under these rules, Naut was found innocent and released.

Angered by the accusations, Naut accused her neighbors of assaulting her, which in turn made the villagers even more determined to find a way to get rid of the troublesome woman. One night, some of them met up secretly at Pye's Mill, not far from the Polhemus Mill, to devise a sinister plan. While they were there, a freak accident resulted in one man being crushed to death by a gigantic two-hundred-pound cloth hammer that fell down on top of him. The meeting came to an abrupt, sobering end, as did plans to rid the neighborhood of Naut, for the schemers were convinced that the witch had caused the accident and were then too afraid to further tempt fate. The alleged witch lived out her rightful life and was buried in a cemetery next to her house. The flour mill where all of the excitement took place ceased operation in the twentieth century. All that remains are the hub of the water wheel, the pond, and the dam . . . and maybe the spirits of the accused and the accuser. A historical marker denotes the site.

Thirteen Days, Thirteen Victims

On November 29, 1895, the entire northwest wall of the Tilly Foster Mine off Route 6 in the town of Southeast collapsed, sending an avalanche of stone over unsuspecting workers at various levels who were carried helplessly into the six-hundred-foot abyss and buried under a hundred tons of rock. It took thirteen days to recover the mangled bodies of the unlucky thirteen who died, because the area remained so unstable. Immediately after the cave-in, surviving miners were offered $25 on top of their usual day's wages to return to the pits in search of more bodies, but they were continually driven out by falling rocks.

Finally, the last of the bodies was uncovered on December 12, just before the State Mine Inspector ordered the work halted and the mine made safe before it would be permitted to reopen. The coroner's jury ruled the disaster an unavoidable accident, likely caused by "recent heavy rains," according to a *New York Times* article. But the Lackawanna Iron and Coal Company of Scranton, Pennsylvania, which acquired the mine in 1879, hardly had time to reopen it. For two years after the mining disaster, an underground spring breached a wall of the pit, and the massive crater eventually filled with water from the Middle Branch Reservoir, part of the Croton Watershed that feeds the New York City water supply.

The mine was named after a previous owner of the property, Tillingham Foster, who died in 1842. When Harvey Iron and Steel Company first opened a mine there in 1853, it attracted many Italian and Irish immigrants to the town of Southeast. The heyday of production of magnetic iron ore at the Tilly Foster Mines was in the 1870s, but it wasn't until 1890, under the direction of Lackawanna Iron and Coal, that the mine was converted into an open pit. The disaster happened five years later, and by 1897, the inundated mine was closed. Though thirteen lives were cut tragically short that horrific November day, it was the quick reactions of sympathetic bystanders who prevented the devastated family members of the victims from becoming further statistics. The *New York Times* of December 1 of that year noted the response to the tragedy:

> The grief of the Italian women was poignant in the extreme and was manifested in an extraordinary manner. Four of these poor women attempted to hurl themselves headlong into the mine. They

were, with difficulty, restrained. They bit their arms savagely so that blood flowed copiously, and with their finger nails, they literally tore the skin from their cheeks in shreds. The mind of one of these unfortunate women gave way under the terrible strain.

Suffice it to say, the Tilly Foster area absorbed some pretty intense, painful emotions from the cave-in. Since the deadly mining accident, mysterious lights and floating orbs have allegedly been seen in and around the pit. Many people believe them to be the spirits of the deceased miners, but some wonder if the area contains a vortex or portal to another dimension because various types of paranormal phenomena have been reportedly seen. Like most Hudson Valley towns, UFOs have been spotted in Brewster and Southeast, but the Tilly Foster Mine area seems especially affected by Bigfoot sightings, encounters with out-of-habitat creatures, and the proverbial close encounters of the third kind. Is it because of the magnetic iron ore deposits? Paranormal researchers believe certain geological conditions, like areas with heavy concentrations of iron ore and quartz deposits, may result in heightened paranormal activity. This whole area, with the Balanced Rock, the Stone Chambers, alien encounters, and UFO sightings on the Magnetic Mine Roads in Brewster, is rife with these types of occurrences.

Whang Hollow Portal

At the end of Whangtown Road in Kent Cliffs, a hamlet of the town of Kent, is a large stone chamber believed to conceivably have been used around 1589 B.C. as an ancient calendar to determine the first day of winter, based on where the chamber opening aligns with the rising sun. It is also known that Native Americans dwelled within the Whang Hollow valley some ten thousand to twelve thousand years before the first European settlers arrived. Inside this mysterious chamber, many people have encountered both benevolent and threatening forces.

In Phil Imbrogno's article "UFOs and the Stone Chambers of New York's Hudson Valley" on *Alien Seeker News* online, he tells of an individual who happened to be passing by the chamber at dusk one evening and noticed a flickering reddish glow coming from within it. As he approached the entrance to see what it might be, the odd light went out, leaving him staring into utter blackness. Trespassing teens, he wondered? He was all alone on his evening walk, and he hadn't seen anyone else nearby. In case someone was there, however, he called out. There was no response. He did hear a generator, or something similar, running, and he heard someone playing a flute. Yet, when he stepped over the threshold, everything became suddenly silent. Undeterred, he ventured in several feet until an invisible force field knocked him off his feet. Whatever it was, it obviously didn't want him intruding, but neither did it want him to leave. When he stood and attempted to escape, he ran into the force field again and was knocked to the ground. This time, looking toward the entrance, he saw a hooded male figure, slightly illuminated, wearing a long robe. The figure calmly pointed at the man as if acknowledging him. Then the figure disappeared and the force field was gone. The man promptly departed. Such apparitions or beings have been reported by many people over the years in the stone chambers throughout Putnam County.

Imbrogno and co-author Marianne Horrigan describe quite a different scenario in their 2005 book, *Celtic Mysteries: Windows to Another Dimension in America's Northeast.* An individual who was brave enough to spend an entire night alone in the same stone chamber on Whangtown Road found himself enveloped in a comforting light as he meditated. In his mind's eye, he sensed a hooded, robed being standing behind him, but unlike the young man who fled the chamber in fear, this man was filled with such a sense of peace that he returned again and again to the same spot. Quite a contrast to being thrown against the wall and onto the floor. Imbrogno speculates in his *Interdimensional Universe* that the stone chambers in the Hudson Valley may have been built thousands of years ago by Celtic explorers and Druid priests, who excelled at identifying locations of portals to parallel universes. Thus, they were able to place their stone chambers and temples in places most conducive to paranormal activity, like sightings and encounters with extraterrestrials, angels, ghosts, Bigfoot, and so on. This begs the following question: Are the many stone chambers of the Hudson Valley actually portals to other worlds? If they are, it would certainly explain why the entire region has been steeped in supernatural tales for centuries.

Bibliography

Books

Hine, Charles G., and Henry Charlton Beck. *The Old Mine Road.* Piscataway, NJ: Rutgers University Press, 1963.

Hynek, J. Allen, Philip J. Imbrogno, and Bob Pratt. *Night Siege: The Hudson Valley UFO Sightings.* Woodbury, MN: Lewellyn Worldwide, 1998.

Imbrogno, Philip. *Interdimensional Universe.* Woodbury, MN: Lewellyn Worldwide, 2008.

Imbrogno, Philip J., and Marianne Horrigan. *Celtic Mysteries: Windows to Another Dimension in America's Northeast.* New York: Cosimo Books, 2005.

Macken, Lynda Lee. *Empire Ghosts: New York State's Haunted Landmarks.* Forked River, NJ: Black Cat Press, 2004.

Menand, L. *Autobiography and Recollections of Incidents Connected with Horticulture Affairs, Etc. from 1807 Up to This Day 1892.* Albany, NY: Weed, Parsons, 1892.

Myers, Arthur. *The Ghostly Register.* Chicago: Contemporary Books, 1986.

Pelletreau, William S. *History of Putnam County, New York.* Philadelphia: W. W. Preston, 1886.

Revai, Cheri. *The Big Book of New York Ghost Stories.* Mechanicsburg, PA: Stackpole Books, 2009.

———. *Haunted New York: Ghosts and Strange Phenomena of the Empire State.* Mechanicsburg, PA: Stackpole Books, 2006.

Skinner, Charles M. *Legends of Our Own Land: The Hudson and Its Hills.* Philadelphia: J. B. Lippincott, 1896.

Smitten, Susan. *Ghosts of New York State.* Auburn, WA: Ghost House Books, 2004.

Streiber, Whitley. *Communion: A True Story.* New York: Avon Books, 1988.

Zimmerman, Linda. *Ghost Investigator, Volume 1: Hauntings of the Hudson Valley.* Rocky Mount, NC: Eagle Press, 2002.

Online Sources
(in order by story)

"Hudson Valley." *Wikipedia*. Retrieved 24 April 2009. http://en.wikipedia .org/wiki/Hudson_Valley.

"Travel Guide to New York's Hudson River Valley." *Hudson Valley Voyager*. Retrieved 24 April 2009. www.hudsonvalleyvoyager.com/Regions/ uv/uv_index.html.

"Cohoes Music Hall." *Cohoes Music Hall*. Retrieved 18 March 2009. http:// cohoesmusichall.com/index.php?option = com_content&view = article &id = 66&Itemid = 77.

"Forest Park Cemetery." *Wikipedia*. Retrieved 27 March 2009. http://en .wikipedia.org/wiki/Forest_Park_Cemetery.

"The Irish Mist." *NNYPRS*. Retrieved 7 February 2009. www.nnyprs.com/ the_irish_mist.htm.

"History of the Building." *The Irish Mist*. Retrieved 15 February 2009. www.theirishmist.com/pages/history.html.

Corsaro, James S. and Kathleen D. Roe. "Labor and Industry in Troy and Cohoes: A Brief History." *University at Albany, State University of New York*. Retrieved 5 March 2009. www.albany.edu/history/Troy-Cohoes.

McGrath, Bill. "Troy's One Hundred Years 1789-1889: Stove Manufacturing." *RootsWeb*. Retrieved 5 March 2009. www.rootsweb.ancestry.com/ ~ nyrensse/troystove.htm.

Somers, Wayne. "Accolades. Did You Know?" *Union College*. Retrieved 30 September 2008. www.union.edu/N/DS/edition_display.php?e = 1445&s = 7328.

Vander Veer, Kathleen. "Alice Vander Veer & royalty, Holland." *Genealogy*. Retrieved 30 September 2008. www.jenforum.org/vandiver/messages/ 696.html.

"The Chronicle: This ghost couldn't wait for Halloween." *Union College*. Retrieved 30 September 2008. www.union.edu/N/DS/edition_display .php?e = 59&s = 4038.

Reynolds, Cuyler. "Hudson-Mohawk Genealogical and Family Memoirs: Vander Veer." *Schenectady Digital History Archive*. Retrieved 24 February 2009. www.schenectadyhistory.org/families/hmgfm/vanderveer-1.html.

"Union College." *Wikipedia*. Retrieved 26 February 2009. http://en .wikipedia.org/wiki/Union_College.

"Mr. Jackson's Garden." *Union College*. Written 1 July 1996. Retrieved 26 February 2009. www.union.edu/N/DS/s.php?s = 2632.

"Harmen Jansen Knickerbocker." *Wikipedia*. Retrieved 15 March 2009. http://en.wikipedia.org/wiki/Harmen_Jansen_Knickerbocker.

"Herman Knickerbocker." *Wikipedia*. Retrieved 15 March 2009. http://en .wikipedia.org/wiki/Herman_Knickerbocker.

"Mansion Restoration." *Knic*. Retrieved 15 March 2009. www.knic.com/ Mansion.htm.

Bibliography

Diane G. "Knickerbocker Mansion." *Grave Addiction*. Retrieved 1 October 2008. www.graveaddiction.com/dgknickm.html.

Sigourney, Lydia. "Schaghticoke and the Knickerbockers." *Knic*. Retrieved 15 March 2009. www.knic.com/Harpers/Harper43.GIF.

Franklin, Kevin. "Re: Joseph Strain Family, NY." *Genealogy*. Retrieved 2 October 2008. http://genforum.genealogy.com/strain/messages/1079.html

"Menands Manor." *Archplanet*. Retrieved 16 February 2009. www.archplanet.org/wiki/Menands_Manor.

"A Benefit Evening at the Haunted Menands Manor." *NY Charities*. Retrieved 3 March 2009. www.nycharities.org/event/event.asp?CE_ID =1854.

"West Hall (Rensselaer Polytechnic Institute)." *Wikipedia*. Retrieved 16 March 2009. http://en.wikipedia.org/wiki/West_Hall_(Rensselaer _Polytechnic_Institute).

"West Hall is being reborn again." *Rensselaer Magazine: Winter 2004: West Hall Revival*. Retrieved 16 March 2009. www.rpi.edu/dept/metasite/ news/magazine/winter2004/feature3-pg2.html.

"McMahon, Bessie." *RootsWeb*. Retrieved 11 December 2007. www.rootsweb .com/~nyrenss2/Troy/3rdward-M.htm.

"Our History." *Ten Broeck Mansion*. Retrieved 2 October 2008. http://sites .google.com/site/tenbroeckmansion/Home/our-history.

"Ten Broeck Uncorked – The Ghosts of Ten Broeck." *Local Wine Events*. Retrieved 2 October 2008. www.localwineevents.com/Albany-Wine/ event-193341.html.

Bielinski, Stefan. "Abraham Ten Broeck." *New York State Museum*. Retrieved 2 October 2008. www.nysm.nysed.gov/Albany/bios/t/abtbroeck6.html.

"Ten Broeck Mansion." *Wikipedia*. Retrieved 2 October 2008. http://en .wikipedia.org/wiki/Ten_Broeck_Mansion

Davenport, Peter. "The Albany International Airport UFO Video." *The UFO Casebook*. Retrieved 22 April 2009. www.ufocasebook.com/Albany.html.

"Albany, NY – Cigar caught on Tape." *ET Reality News*. Retrieved 23 April 2009. www.geocities.com/jilaens/worldarc02.htm?200923.

Trainor, Joseph. "UFO Videotaped in Upstate New York." *UFO Roundup*. Retrieved 23 April 2009. www.ufoinfo.com/roundup/v07/rnd0744 .shtml.

"Q: UFO Sighting Shown on CNN." *Google Answers*. Retrieved 23 April 2009. http://answers.google.com/answers/threadview?id=89928.

"Claudius Smith's Den." *NY, NJ, CT Botany*. Retrieved 26 February 2009. http://nynjctbotany.org/whudson/nyclauds.html.

"Claudius Smith." *Ghosts of Ohio*. Retrieved 2 April 2009. www.geocities .com/ghosts_of_oh/Claudius.html?20092.

"1841 Goshen Courthouse." *Wikipedia*. Retrieved 2 April 2009. http://en .wikipedia.org/wiki/1841_Goshen_Courthouse.

Heselton, Lil. "Claudius Smith: Fact and Fiction." *Genealogy Rootsweb*. Retrieved 26 February 2009. http://freepages.genealogy.rootsweb.ancestry.com/ ~ frederick/docs/CSmithfact&fiction.htm.

"Claudius Smith: Loyalist Cowboy of the Ramapos." *UELAC*. Retrieved 26 February 2009. www.uelac.org/Loyalist-Trails/2007/Loyalist-Trails-2007 .php?issue = 200713.

"Interments in the Christ Church Cemetery." *RootsWeb*. Retrieved 12 March 2009. www.rootsweb.ancestry.com/ ~ nydutche/cems/chrichu.htm.

"Elting Memorial Library." *Wikipedia*. Retrieved 15 February 2009. http:// en.wikipedia.org/wiki/Elting_Memorial_Library.

"Library Ghosts: Northeastern U.S./Britannica Blog." *Britannica*. Retrieved 8 January 2009. www.britannica.com/blogs/2008/10/library-ghosts -northeastern-us/.

"Mrs. Edward Schoonmaker." *NYTimes Search*. Retrieved 23 February 2009. http://query.nytimes.com/search/sitesearch?query = %22elting + memorial + library%22.

"About the Elting Library." *Elting Library*. Retrieved 15 February 2009. www.eltinglibrary.org/about.html.

"Estimated New York Public Library Construction Needs 2006: Profiles." *NYSL*. Retrieved 23 February 2009. www.nysl.nysed.gov/libdev/ construc/profiles.htm.

"Elting Library Ghost Cam." *Record Online*. Retrieved 15 February 2009. www.recordonline.com/apps/pbcs.dll/article?AID = /20080321/MEDIA0 201/80321036.

"New Paltz: Haunted Library and More." *Pennsylvania Haunts and History*. Retrieved 16 February 2009. http://hauntsandhistory.blogspot.com/ 2008/07/new-paltz-haunted-library-and-more.html.

"The Fort Decker Museum of History." *Minisink Valley Historical Society*. Retrieved 1 October 2008. www.minisink.org/forthist.html.

"The City of Port Jervis." *Upper Delaware Scenic Byway: History*. Retrieved 1 October 2008. www.upperdelawarescenicbyway.org/history/towns/ portjervis/portjervis.php.

"History of Port Jervis." *NY NJ CT Botany*. Retrieved 15 March 2009. www.nynjctbotany.org/whudson/portjervishistory.html.

"Cragsmoor, New York." *Answers*. Retrieved 15 February 2009. www.answers .com/topic/cragsmoor-new-york.

"Ice Caves Mountain." *Show Caves of the United States of America*. Retrieved 15 February 2009. www.showcaves.com/English/usa/ showcaves/IceCaves.html.

"Report #8064 (Class A): Ulster County, 1985 Winter Hike Leads to Encounter with Large Bipedal Creature." *Bigfoot Field Researchers Organization*. Retrieved 15 February 2009. www.bfro.net/GDB/ show_report.asp?ID = 8064.

"The Landscape. Minisink Valley Historical Society: Port Jervis and the Gilded Age." *Minisink Valley Historical Society*. Retrieved 6 March 2009. www.minisink.org/histpj.html.

Bibliography

"Laurel Grove Cemetery." *Upper Delaware Scenic Byway: History*. Retrieved 2 October 2008. www.upperdelawarescenicbyway.org/history/towns/portjervis/portjervis.php.

"Laurel Grove Cemetery." *TSPR Ghosts*. Retrieved 2 October 2008. www.tsprghosts.com/Laurel%20Grove1.htm.

"Social Problems of the Era." *Minisink Valley Historical Society*. Retrieved 6 March 2009. www.minisink.org/histpj.html.

"Martin Van Buren National Historic Site." *Wikipedia*. Retrieved 2 October 2008. http://en.wikipedia.org/wiki/Martin_Van_Buren_National_Historic_Site.

"Village of Kinderhook 1609-1976." *Kinderhook Connection*. Retrieved 2 October 2008. www.kinderhookconnection.com/history2.htm.

"Welcome to Old Dutch Church." *Old Dutch Church*. Retrieved 2 October 2008. www.olddutchchurch.org.

Werner, James W. "The Old Dutch Church, Kingston, New York." *J. W. Werner*. Retrieved 2 October 2008. http://home.att.net/ ~ jwwerner51/OldDutchChurch.html.

"Hobgoblin." *Wikipedia*. Retrieved 4 March 2009. http://en.wikipedia.org/wiki/Hobgoblin.

"Pine Bush, New York." *Wikipedia*. Retrieved 22 April 2009. http://en.wikipedia.org/wiki/Pine_Bush,_NY.

"Bannerman Castle." *Lost in Jersey*. Retrieved 12 March 2009. www.lostinjersey.com/historic/bannerman.html.

"Near Bannerman's Island, Tale of a Shelled Killer." *Mysteries of the Hudson Valley, 1995–1996*. Retrieved 12 March 2009. www.beaconite.com/hudsonvalley.html.

"Frequently Asked Questions: Behavior (Bigfoot)." *Bigfoot Field Researchers Organization*. Retrieved 1 April 2009. http://bfro.net/gdb/show_FAQ.asp?id = 587.

"Report #7514 (Class B)." *Bigfoot Field Researchers Organization*. Retrieved 1 April 2009. http://bfro.net/gdb/show_FAQ.asp?id = 7514.

"The Doug Pridgen Footage (a.k.a. the "New York Baby Footage")." *Bigfoot Field Researchers Organization*. Retrieved 1 April 2009. http://bfro.net/news/nybaby.asp.

"Plattekill (town), New York." *Wikipedia*. Retrieved 1 April 2009. http://en.wikipedia.org/wiki/Plattekill_(town),_New_York.

"Modena, New York." *Wikipedia*. Retrieved 1 April 2009. http://en.wikipedia.org/wiki/Modena,_NY.

Stefko, Jill. "Ghosts of West Point, USMA." *Suite 101*. Retrieved 5 January 2009. http://ghosts-hauntings.suite101.com/article.cfm/ghosts_of_west_point_usma.

"Ghosts." *West-Point*. Retrieved 5 January 2009. www.west-point.org/family/bicent/ghosts.html.

"Project Blue Book." *Wikipedia*. Retrieved 24 April 2009. http://en.wikipedia.org/wiki/Project_Blue_Book.

"The Bible UFO Connection: UFO Quotations: United States Military Officers." *Bible UFO*. Retrieved 24 April 2009. www.bibleufo.com/zquotemil.htm.

"Twining, General Nathan Farragut (1897-1982)." *The Internet Encyclopedia of Science*. Retrieved 24 April 2009. www.daviddarling.info/encyclopedia/T/Twining.html.

"Nathan Farragut Twining." *Wikipedia*. Retrieved 24 April 2009. http://en.wikipedia.org/wiki/Nathan_Twining.

"Interview with Stan Friedman on UFOs and Roswell." *UFO Evidence*. Retrieved 24 April 2009. www.ufoevidence.org/documents/doc69.htm.

"George S. Brown." *NNDB*. Retrieved 24 April 2009. www.nndb.com/people/591/000172075/.

"MacArthur, Douglas, General." *Ufologie*. Retrieved 24 April 2009. www.ufologie.net/htm/m.htm.

Vernon, Alex. "Ghost Stories." *American Heritage*. Retrieved 30 September 2008. www.americanheritage.com/articles/magazine/ah/2002/5/2002_5_64.shtml.

"Thayer Home." *Haunted Houses*. Retrieved 5 January 2009. www.hauntedhouses.com/states/ny/Thayer_home.cfm.

"Exploring New York from a Different Side (Part 1)." *Buzzle*. Retrieved 18 February 2009. www.buzzle.com/articles/exploring-new-york-from-a-different-side-part-1.html.

"Quarters 100." *Tour of West Point*. Retrieved 23 March 2009. www.westpoint.edu/tour/Quarters100.asp.

"Sylvanus Thayer." *Wikipedia*. Retrieved 22 March 2009. http://en.wikipedia.org/wiki/Sylvanus_Thayer.

"United States Military Academy." *Wikipedia*. Retrieved 8 April 2009. http://en.wikipedia.org/wiki/United_States_Military_Academy.

"Stambovsky v. Ackley." *Wikipedia*. Retrieved 8 April 2009. http://en.wikipedia.org/wiki/Stambovsky_v._Ackley.

Untitled (regarding Balanced Rock). *SPACE*. Retrieved 18 February 2009. http://community-2.webtv.net/HEgeln/SPACESearchProject/page4.html.

"Megalith." *Wikipedia*. Retrieved 22 April 2009. http://en.wikipedia.org/wiki/Megalith.

"Dolmen." *Wikipedia*. Retrieved 22 April 2009. http://en.wikipedia.org/wiki/Dolmen.

"North Salem, New York." *Wikipedia*. Retrieved 22 April 2009. http://en.wikipedia.org/wiki/North_Salem,_New_York.

"The Balanced Rock: Town of North Salem, NY." *Waymarking*. Retrieved 21 April 2009. www.waymarking.com/waymarks/WM3099.

"List of Sacred Power Sites in the United States." *Above Top Secret*. Retrieved 21 April 2009. www.abovetopsecret.com/forum/thread193711/pg1

Bibliography

"UFOs and Other Phenomena." *Alien Seeker News*. Retrieved 18 February 2009. www.alienseekernews.com/articles/ufos-and-stone-chambers .html.

"The Bird and Bottle Inn." *The Bird and Bottle Inn*. Retrieved 2 October 2008. www.thebirdandbottleinn.com/

"Emily Warren Roebling." *Wikipedia*. Retrieved 2 October 2008. http://en .wikipedia.org/wiki/Emily_Warren_Roebling.

"Happy Birthday to the Brooklyn Bridge." *Hudson Valley Travel Guide*. Retrieved 15 February 2009. http://visithudsonvalley.blogspot.com/ 2008/05/happy-125th-birthday-to-brooklyn-bridge.html.

"The Bird & Bottle Inn." *Frommer's*. Retrieved 15 February 2009. www.frommers.com/destinations/lowerhudsonvalley/H48622.html.

"The Hudson Valley UFO Sightings." *UFO Help Files*. Retrieved 24 April 2009. www.ufohelpfiles.com/Hudson.htm.

Nicoletti, Linda. "The Hudson Valley UFO Flap: The Sightings of the Night of March 17, 1983, in Brewster." *Ufologie*. Retrieved 24 April 2009. www.ufologie.net/hv/hudson17mar1983.htm.

"Close Encounters of the Make Contact Kind . . . Contact of the 5th Kind in the Hudson Valley." *SPACE*. Retrieved 18 February 2009. http:// community-2.webtv.net/HEgeln/SPACESearchProject/page4.html.

"The 'Ghost' of the Depot . . . Only Two Minutes from the Train." *Cold Spring Depot*. Retrieved 15 February 2009. http://coldspringdepot .com/depot2.htm.

"Cold Spring (Metro-North station)." *Wikipedia*. Retrieved 22 February 2009. http://en.wikipedia.org/wiki/Cold_Spring_(Metro-North_station).

"Cold Spring Depot Restaurant." *Restaurants: Philipstown/Cold Spring*. Retrieved 22 February 2009. www.hvgateway.com/CSDEPOT.htm.

"The Masters School." *Wikipedia*. Retrieved 1 October 2008. http://en .wikipedia.org/wiki/The_Masters_School.

"Estherwood (Dobbs Ferry, New York)." *Wikipedia*. Retrieved 1 October 2008. http://en.wikipedia.org/wiki/Estherwood_(Dobbs_Ferry,_ New_York).

Imbrogno, Philip J. "Incident at Indian Point." *Capitol Hill*. Retrieved 30 September 2008. www.geocities.com/CapitolHill/Lobby/8979/ page18.html.

Cooper, Vicki. "Incident at Indian Point Reactor Complex, N.Y. 1984." *Pine Bush UFO*. Retrieved 30 September 2008. www.pinebushufo.com/ pinebushpage56.htm.

"Indian Point Energy Center." *Wikipedia*. Retrieved 30 September 2008. http://en.wikipedia.org/wiki/Indian_Point_Energy_Center.

"The Indian Point Nuclear Power Plants: A History of Failure, Mishaps, Secrecy & Lies." *Capitol Hill*. Retrieved 6 March 2009. www.geocities .com/CapitolHill/Lobby/8979/page 4.html?20096.

"The Ten Most Compelling UFO Cases in History in Order of Compelling- ness." *Paranormal*. Retrieved 9 March 2009. http://paranormal.se/ mirror/bbs_textiles/ufo/SIGHTINGS/10best.ufo.

Mathew and Helena. "A Spooky Story for October." *Mathew and Helena Blog Spot*. Retrieved 2 October 2008. http://mathewandhelena.blogspot .com/2007/10/spooky-story-for-October.html.

Barker, Vicki, Marie Koestler, and Michael Secora. "Rockland County Cemeteries, Volume 1: Clarkstown." *Rockland Genealogy*. Retrieved 16 February 2009. http://rocklandgenealogy.org/cemetery_intro.htm.

Ly, Laura. "'Gael Winds' Scholastic Newspaper Interviews Dr. MacGuffie." *SHARE*. Retrieved 16 February 2009. http://shareafrica.org/articles/ gael-winds-scholastic-newsletter-interviews-dr-macguffie.

"Black panther." *Wikipedia*. Retrieved 20 March 2009. http://en.wikipedia .org/wiki/Black_panther.

Aiello, Tony. "Mysterious Big Black Cats Shock Rockland County." *WCBSTV*. Retrieved 20 March 2009. http://wcbstv.com/local/ mysterious.big.cats.2.963467.html.

"Black Cat." *Wikipedia*. Retrieved 20 March 2009. http://en.wikipedia.org/ wiki/Black_cat.

"Stone Chambers: Native Temples." *Native Stones*. Retrieved 18 February 2009. www.nativestones.com/chambers.htm.

Imbrogno, Philip. "UFOs and the Stone Chambers of New York's Hudson Valley." *Alien Seeker News*. Retrieved 18 February 2009. www .alienseekernews.com/articles/ufos-and-stone-chambers.html.

"Unusual Sites in Putnam County, NY: The Stone Chambers." *Think About It*. Retrieved 30 September 2008. www.think-aboutit.com/Underground/ Ellenville_tunnels_and_pine_bush.htm.

"Smalley's Inn and Restaurant." *Wikipedia*. Retrieved 26 March 2009. http://en.wikipedia.org/wiki/Smalley%27s_Inn_%26_Restaurant.

Untitled (re: Spook Rock). *Discovering Rockland Exhibit*. Retrieved 18 February 2009. www2.lhric.org/virmus2/BYKIDS/texts.html.

"No Rest for the Eerie." *CCSD*. Retrieved 18 February 2009. www.ccsd.edu/ north/publication/pdf/1999_oct.pdf

Frizzle. "Gravity Hills." *Gravity Hills*. Retrieved 24 February 2009. http:// userpages.umbc.edu/ ~ frizzell/gravhills.html.

"Gravity Hill." *Wikipedia*. Retrieved 24 February 2009. http://en.wikipedia .org/wiki/Gravity_hill.

"Spook's On in Rockland County." *Rockland Cast*. Retrieved 2 October 2008. www.rocklandcast.com.

"Irvington, New York." *Wikipedia*. Retrieved 3 April 2009. http://en.wikipedia.org/wiki/Irvington,_New_York.

"Sunnyside (Tarrytown, New York)." *Wikipedia*. Retrieved 13 March 2009. http://en.wikipedia.org/wiki/Sunnyside_(Tarrytown,_New_York).

"Washington Irving." *Wikipedia*. Retrieved 13 March 2009. http://en .wikipedia.org/wiki/Washington_Irving.

"The Legend of Sleepy Hollow." *Wikipedia*. Retrieved 13 March 2009. http://en.wikipedia.org/wiki/The_Legend_of_Sleepy_Hollow.

"Washington Irving's Sunnyside." *Hudson Valley*. Retrieved 3 April 2009. www.hudsonvalley.org/content/view/13/43/.

Bibliography

"Sunnyside." *American Memory from the Library of Congress*. Retrieved 3
   April 2009. http://memory.loc.gov/cgi-bin/query/r?ammem/hh:@
   field(NUMBER + @band(NY0876).

Eberhart, George. "Haunted Libraries in the U.S.: Nebraska-Oregon."
   (Tarrytown, Sunnyside.) *Britannica*. Retrieved 13 March 2009. www
   .britannica.com/blogs/2007/10/haunted-libraries-in-the-us-nebraska
   -oregon.

"Y's Arn's History of Meteorites." *Meteorites 4 Sale*. www.meteorites4sale
   .net/MET_Y.HTM.

"(Meteorobs) FYI More Ripley's Believe It or Not Meteors/Meteorites."
   Meteorobs. Retrieved 9 March 2009. www.meteorobs.org/maillist/
   msg290004.html.

Reisman, Phil. "Stop, Hey What's That Sound?" *LoHud*. Retrieved 29 March
   2009. http://reisman.lohudblogs.com/2009/03/12/stop-hey-whats
   -that-sound/.

―――. "Things That Go Boom in the Night." *LoHud*. Retrieved 29 March
   2009. http://reisman.lohudblogs.com/2009/03/12/things-that
   -go-boom-in-the-night/.

"Big Boom in White Plains May Have Been Meteorite." *WCBSTV*. Retrieved
   9 March 2009. http://wcbstv.com/local/loud.boom.meteorite.2
   .953611.html.

Hamilton, Rosanna L. "Meteoroids and Meteorites." *Solar Views*. Retrieved
   9 March 2009. www.solarviews.com/eng/meteor.htm.

Graham, Keith P. "More on the Polhemus Grist Mill: The Clarksville Witch."
   Wanderings. Retrieved 1 March 2009. www.cthreepo.com/blog/2006/
   05/more-on-polhemus-grist-mill.html.

"Declark-Polhemus Mill." *Rockland County, New York Historical Sites and
   Landmarks*. Retrieved 1 March 2009. www.rootsweb.ancestry.com/
   ~ nyrockla/history.htm.

"West Nyack, New York." *Wikipedia*. Retrieved 1 March 2009. http://en
   .wikipedia.org/wiki/West_Nyack.

"Old Mill." *I Spy in West Nyack*. Retrieved 1 March 2009. www.rcls.org/
   ispy/wny/index.htm.

"Tilly Foster Mine." *Wikipedia*. Retrieved 30 September 2008. http://en
   .wikipedia.org/wiki/Tilly_Foster_Mine.

"Tilly Foster Mine." *Southeast Museum*. Retrieved 30 September 2008.
   www.southeastmuseum.org./SE_Tour99/SE_Tour/html/tilly_foster
   _mine.htm.

"Brewster Mine Drainage Tunnel?" *Iron Miners*. Retrieved 24 February 2009.
   http://www.ironminers.com/mineforum/viewtopic.php?t
   = 20076&sid = 915a0ab5b38dbb60d860cba5f370b8b3.

AlienCat. "Weird and Strange: Abandoned Mines." *Mystery Planet*.
   Retrieved 30 September 2008. http://groups.msn.com/mysteryplanet/
   weirdstrange.msnw?

"Struck by an Unseen Force." *Alien Seeker News*. Retrieved 18 February 2009. www.alienseekernews.com/articles/ufos-and-stone-chambers .html.

"Whang Hollow." *Wikipedia*. Retrieved 21 April 2009. http://en.wikipedia .org/wiki/Whang_Hollow.

Magazine and Newspaper Articles
(*in order by story*)

Gray, John. "John Gray: Nothing Like a Good Ghost Story." *Troy Record*, 29 October 2008.

Barton, Christine. "Forest Park Cemetery Filled with Ghostly Tales." *Troy Record*, 31 October 2008.

Scanlon, John. "Scanlon: Irish Mist to Replace Lindy's." *Troy Record*, 20 May 2001.

"New Restaurant at Historic Troy Site." *Business Review* (Albany), 6 August 2001.

"Obituaries (Millard E. Rosenthal)." *Troy Record*, 29 April 2007.

"Our State Institutions, XXIV." *New York Times*, 12 February 1872.

Gilbert, Kevin. "Turn of the Century Chronicle." *Troy Record*, 28 January 2002.

Ritter, Don. "'Knick' in Time." *Troy Record*, 12 October 2004.

Viele, General Egbert L. "The Knickerbockers of New York Two Centuries Ago." *Harper's Monthly Magazine*, December 1876.

"Louis Menand." *New York Times*, 16 August 1900.

Menand, Howard. "History of Menands." *Village of Menands, 50th Anniversary*. n.p., 1974.

Franco, James V. "What is Haunting Menands Manor?" *Troy Record*, 25 July 2008.

"Fire Does $10,000,000 Damage to New York's Great State Capital." *San Antonio Light*, 29 March 1911.

"Many Millions Loss in New York Capitol Fire." *Daily Review*, 29 March 1911.

Barnes, Steve. "Capitol Ghost-Busting Yields the Unexplained." *Albany Times Union*, 30 October 1997.

"Albany Capitol Ruined by Fire." *Warren Evening Mirror*, 29 March 1911.

"Capitol Fire-Swept; Pride of the State is Quickly a Wreck." *Syracuse Post-Standard*, 30 March 1911.

"Body Recovered: Samuel Abbott, Victim of Capitol Fire in Albany." *Lowell Sun*, 31 March 1911.

"Run Over by Express Train." *New York Times*, 5 September 1899.

"Beat a Hospital Patient." *New York Times*, 10 July 1897.

Bibliography

Heins, Frances Ingraham. "It Was a Dark and Scary Night: An Intrepid Tour Group Visits Some Local Haunts on the Trail of the Supernatural." *Albany Times Union*, 27 October 2002.

"Deeds of the Cow-Boys." *New York Times*, 23 November 1879.

"Mr. Tower's Church Gift." *New York Times*, 18 July 1888.

Foderaro, Lisa W. "The Librarians Call It an Anomaly (It Wasn't Rattling Chains)." *New York Times*, 20 April 2008.

Horrigan, Jeremiah. "Mystery Haunts Elting Library, 'Ghost' Caught on Videotape." *Times Herald-Record*, 25 March 2008.

"Possible Ghost Sighting at the Elting Library: Is Oscar Still There?" *Hasbrouck Family Association Journal*, June 2008.

"Vander Burgh." (Obituary). *New York Times*, 13 October 1910.

"Carried Over Passaic Falls." *New York Times*, 1 May 1889.

"Built Gallows for Himself." *New York Times*, 9 April 1898.

"The Erie Slaughter." *New York Times*, 17 April 1868.

"The Erie Slaughter." *New York Times*, 21 April 1868.

"The Erie Slaughter." *New York Times*, 4 May 1868.

"Arrested at a Funeral." *New York Times*, 14 February 1892.

"A German Girl's Love and Sad Fate." *New York Times*, 26 December 1881.

"Funeral of Ex-President Van Buren." *New York Times*, 29 July 1862.

"Sale of 'Lindenwald.'" *New York Times*, 17 November 1873.

"Gov. Clinton's Body Rests in Old Home." *New York Times*, 31 May 1908.

"Kingston's Old Cemetery." *New York Times*, 10 June 1894.

"Church 250 Years Old." *New York Times*, 4 April 1909.

Rodell, Susanna. "Editorial Notebook: Bannerman's Folly; A Hudson Island, Haunted by Goblins." *New York Times*, 20 January 1996.

"F. Bannerman, Arms Dealer, Dies." *New York Times*, 28 November 1918.

"Explosion Wrecks Bannerman Arsenal." *New York Times*, 16 August 1920.

"A Strange Sentence." *Auburn Citizen*, 7 January 1908.

Horrigan, Jeremiah. "Seeing Sasquatch." *Times Herald-Record*, 24 November 2005.

"Academy Denies 'Ghost' Is Hoax." *Times Herald-Record*, 16 November 1972.

Corry, John. "Navy Calls West Point Ghost Ploy in Old Army Game." *New York Times*, 30 November 1972.

"Army Puts West Point Ghost Room Off-Limits." *Pasco East Newspaper*, 17 November 1972.

Members of USMA Company G-3. "A Modest Report." *Pointer* [newsletter], December 1972.

"Phantom of the Point." *Time*, 4 December 1972.

Warren, Ed, Lorraine Warren, and Robert Chase. "Ghost Hunters Discover JFK's Spirit Haunting a Home at West Point." *National Enquirer*, date unknown.

James, Alexa. "Ghost Stories Fly at West Point. Something's in Those Rooms." *Times Herald-Record*, 31 October 2008.

McFadden, Robert D. "A Ghostly Cavalryman Reports for Duty at West Point." *New York Times*, 21 November 1972.

Claus, Nancy L. "North Salem's Balanced Rock: A Geological Mystery." *Westchester Magazine*, March 2006.

MacDonald, Don. "No Greater Love." *Putnam County News and Recorder*, 15 October 2003.

Prevost, Lisa. "If You're Thinking of Living in Cold Spring, N.Y.; Historic, Rustic, and on the Hudson." *New York Times*, 15 August 1999.

Reed, M. H. "Famished and Footsore? Stops along a Road Trip." *New York Times*, 24 June 2007.

Stern, Lea Lane. "Leisure, Good Food, and a Place to Nap After." *New York Times*, 31 December 2000.

"J. Jennings McComb Dead." *New York Times*, 1 April 1901.

"The Will Filed of James Jennings M'Comb." *New York Times*, 14 April 1901.

"Herzog Will Not Discuss McComb Will." *New York Times*, 16 April 1901.

"J. J. McComb's Will Proved: Divides $15,000,000 or More among the Heirs, Daughter Better Off If She Does Not Marry." *New York Times*, 23 April 1901.

Untitled Obituary (Mary Esther McComb). *New York Times*, 2 July 1901.

"Mrs. Mary E. McComb Dead, The Widow of J. Jennings McComb, Whose Strange Will Attracted Public Attention." *New York Times*, 3 July 1901.

"McComb Will Contest, Daughter of Testator Fights Clause Forbidding Her Marrying Her Sweetheart." *New York Times*, 27 November 1901.

"Miss M'Comb Now Mrs. Lewis Herzog, Risked Millions in Inheritance for Her Affections' Sake." *New York Times*, 1 January 1902.

"Mrs. Herzog Wins Wealth." *New York Times*, 24 March 1903.

"Mystery in Death of Banker at Sea." *New York Times*, 28 December 1903.

"Reticent on Trouble that Made Garth Ill." *New York Times*, 29 December 1903.

"Some Garth Rumors Denied, Mrs. Garth Still Silent." *New York Times*, 30 December 1903.

"Successor to Mr. Garth: Move to Have His Place as McComb Estate Executor Filled." *New York Times*, 31 December 1903.

"McComb Estate Accounting." *New York Times*, 27 March 1904.

"Mrs. Garth Owns the Farm, Her Coachman Deeded It Over Before Mr. Garth Died." *New York Times*, 8 April 1904.

Fuchs, Marek. "County Lines; Wedding Bell Blues." *New York Times*, 9 September 2001.

Fabricant, Florence. "Food Stuff." *New York Times*, 14 October 1998.

Sunquist, Fiona. "Malaysian Mystery Leopards." *National Wildlife Magazine*. December/January 2007.

Pollak, Michael. "Stone Chambers Silent on Their Makers." *New York Times*, 16 July 1995.

Kilgannon, Corey. "Putnam's Mysterious Chambers of Stone." *New York Times*, 22 April 2001.

Hanley-Goff, M. J. "Ghost encounters with the Hudson Valley Paranormal Investigations." *Times Herald-Record*, 19 October 2007.

Bibliography

"Daniel Drew's Old Home: The Village of Carmel and Its Surroundings." *New York Times*, 9 November 1890.

"Find a Mrs. Lane Living in Carmel." *New York Times*, 26 September 1919.

"Main Street's Isolated Appearance." *Putnam County Courier*, 20 February 1925.

Nicholson, Dale. "Mythic River: Legends, Ghosts, and Spectral Events in the Hudson Valley." *Columbia County History and Heritage*, Spring 2005.

Tucker, Libby. "Put Your Car in Neutral." *Voices: The Journal of New York Folklore*, Spring/Summer 2006.

"Lifestyle: Sunday Outing; Sunnyside, Where Ghost Stories Were Born." *New York Times*, 21 October 1990.

Bryant, William Cullen. "Washington Irving: Commemoration of the Birth and Death of the Great Historian: Eulogy Delivered Before the New York Historical Society." *New York Times*, 4 April 1860.

Hauser, Christine. "Unexplained Boom Is Reported on Staten Island." *New York Times*, 18 March 2009.

Selkirk, Katie. "Rockland Ghosts Haunt Books, History." *Ram's Horn*, October 1999.

"Twelve Miners Killed." *New York Times*, 30 November 1895.

"Coroner's Jury Blames No One: The Accident at Tilly Foster Mine Unavoidable." *New York Times*, 5 December 1895.

"Thirteen Were Killed." *New York Times*, 1 December 1895.

"Last of the Victims Recovered." *New York Times*, 13 December 1895.

Other Sources

E-mail, between James O'Connor and Shara McGowan regarding O'Connor's experience in 1972 Room 4714 incident, 22 October 2004.

E-mail, between Cheri Farnsworth and Cadet Cpl. Theodore Hoham, 9 April 2009.

Information Office, United States Military Academy. "Fact Sheet—Ghost Story Update" [statement regarding ghost in Room 4714], December 1972.

McGowan, Shara. "Ghost Notes" [notes for West Point Ghost Tour], date unknown.

Memorandum, Lt. Gen. William A. Knowlton, USMA superintentent to Egon Weiss, USMA librarian, 25 October 1972.

Memorandum, Egon Weiss, USMA librarian, to Lt. Gen. William A. Knowlton, USMA superintendent, re: Quarters 100, 3 November 1972.

Official Disposition Form, from Mr. Tozeski, USMA archives chief, to Egon Weiss, USMA librarian, re: Quarters 100, 3 November 1972.

Acknowledgments

MY FAMILY DESERVES THE MOST GRATITUDE, OF COURSE, FOR BEARING with me and letting me do my own thing, as time-consuming as it often is. I'm even more grateful that just seeing and being with each of you negates the effects this kind of research would have on me otherwise. To my husband, Leland Farnsworth, and my daughters, Nicole, Katie, Jamie, and Michelle Revai, thank you for keeping me in this moment and reminding me how precious and good life is. When I'm writing about dark and stormy nights, you brighten my days. And I love you for that.

A big shout-out goes to the other VIPs in my life: my parents, Tom and Jean Dishaw; my brother, Tom Dishaw; my sisters, Cindy Barry and Chris Walker (along with Ed, Rachel, Ryan, Danon, Heather, Amanda, Bryan, Lindsey, and "Baby Walker"); and my in-laws, Carol and Lee Farnsworth. You guys are the best.

This book would not have been possible without the help of quite a few people who offered their personal experiences, recollections of others' experiences, suggestions for stories to research, and information garnered from investigations or other sources. So, in random order, a big, hearty thank you goes to Cadet Cpl. Theodore Hoham of West Point, Cindy and Sal Nicosia of the Shanley Hotel, Merrill McKee and his Northern New York Paranormal Research Society, Central New York's IMOVES, Anthony "Tony" Porto Jr. of Smalley's Inn, Jason Adams of the Bardavon 1869 Opera House, Mitch and Kevin S. (ghost hunters extraordinaire), and Charles Pemburn of Professor Java's Coffee Sanctuary. Thank you all for your time and patience.

To Kyle Weaver and Brett Keener at Stackpole Books, thank you for your faith in me. This is my sixth book with you. I really appreciate your continued interest in my work and value your expertise, friendship, and professionalism.

About the Author

CHERI FARNSWORTH, UNDER THE NAME CHERI REVAI, IS THE AUTHOR OF *The Big Book of New York Ghost Stories* and four other titles in Stackpole's Haunted Series: *Haunted Massachusetts, Haunted Connecticut, Haunted New York,* and *Haunted New York City.* Farnsworth lives in upstate New York with her husband, daughters, and a houseful of pets. She enjoys researching the link between history and the paranormal and has traveled extensively to every nook and cranny of her beloved home state to gather traditional and new stories of ghosts and other strange phenomena. Her Web site at www.theghostauthor.com provides more information on her books and upcoming projects.